SOVIET BOOK PUBLISHING POLICY

SOVIET AND EAST EUROPEAN STUDIES

Books in the series

A. Boltho *Foreign Trade Criteria in Socialist Economies*
Sheila Fitzpatrick *The Commissariat of Enlightenment*
Donald Male *Russian Peasant Organisation before Collectivisation*
P. Wiles, ed. *The Prediction of Communist Economic Performance*
Vladimir V. Kusin *The Intellectual Origins of the Prague Spring*
Galia Golan *The Czechoslovak Reform Movement*
Naum Jasny *Soviet Economists of the Twenties*
Asha L. Datar *India's Economic Relations with the USSR and Eastern Europe, 1953–1969*
T. M. Podolski *Socialist Banking and Monetary Control*
Rudolf Bićanić *Economic Policy in Socialist Yugoslavia*
S. Galai *Liberation in Russia*
Richard B. Day *Leon Trotsky and the Politics of Economic Isolation*
G. Hosking *The Russian Constitutional Experiment: Government and Duma 1907–14*
A. Teichova *An Economic Background to Munich*
J. Ciechanowski *The Warsaw Rising of 1944*
Edward A. Hewett *Foreign Trade Prices in the Council for Mutual Economic Assistance*
Daniel F. Calhoun *The United Front: the TUC and the Russians 1923–28*
Galia Golan *Yom Kippur and After: the Soviet Union and the Middle East Crisis*
Maureen Perrie *The Agrarian Policy of the Russian Socialist-Revolutionary Party from its origins through the revolution of 1905–1907*
Gabriel Gorodetsky *The Precarious Truce: Anglo-Soviet Relations 1924–27*
Paul Vyšný *Neo-Slavism and the Czechs 1898–1914*
James Riordan *Sport in Soviet Society: Development of Sport and Physical Education in Russia and the USSR*

SOVIET
BOOK PUBLISHING
POLICY

—

GREGORY WALKER

Head of Slavonic Section, Bodleian Library, Oxford

CAMBRIDGE UNIVERSITY PRESS

CAMBRIDGE

LONDON · NEW YORK · MELBOURNE

Published by the Syndics of the Cambridge University Press
The Pitt Building, Trumpington Street, Cambridge CB2 1RP
Bentley House, 200 Euston Road, London NW1 2DB
32 East 57th Street, New York, NY 10022, USA
296 Beaconsfield Parade, Middle Park, Melbourne 3206, Australia

© Cambridge University Press 1978

First published 1978

Printed in Great Britain by
Western Printing Services Ltd, Bristol

Library of Congress Cataloguing in Publication Data

Walker, Gregory
Soviet book publishing policy

(Soviet and East European studies)
Bibliography: p.
Includes index.
1. Publishers and publishing – Russia. 2. Book
industries and trade – Russia. I. Title. II. Series.
Z366. W34   658.8′09′0705730947   77–12543
ISBN 0 521 21843 8

Contents

	Acknowledgments	ix
	Glossary of specialised terms	xi
	Note on transliteration	xv
	References to journals and series	xv
1	**Introduction**	**1**
1.1	The study of Soviet book publishing	1
1.2	Soviet publishing policy and the present work	2
1.3	Materials used	4
2	**The political and economic view of Soviet publishing**	**6**
2.1	Publishing as production	6
2.2	Demand and pricing policy	9
2.3	Profits and subsidies	11
2.4	Quality, effectiveness and optimality	13
2.5	The power of the reader	15
3	**The Communist Party**	**18**
3.1	The Central Committee and Department of Propaganda	18
3.2	The Party in the publishing-house	22
3.3	The Party in printing and the book trade	24
3.4	The Party as publisher	25
3.5	The Party's exercise of its authority	26
4	**The government apparatus**	**28**
4.1	The highest organs of government	28
4.2	The State Committee for Publishing	29
4.3	Republic and local publishing administration	36
4.4	Other participating organs	37
4.5	The coordination process	39
4.6	The planning cycle	41

4.7	Automated systems in publishing administration	44
5	**The publishing-house**	**48**
5.1	The publishing-house and its superior organisation	48
5.2	The director and editorial staff	49
5.3	Editorial councils	51
5.4	The economic position of the publishing-house	53
5.5	Selection and handling of manuscripts	55
5.6	Salaries and incentives	59
5.7	Internal planning decisions	62
5.8	Edition sizes	63
5.9	Censorship	65
6	**The author**	**68**
6.1	The author's rights	68
6.2	Contracts between author and publishing-house	69
6.3	Authors' fees	72
6.4	The author, translation and publication abroad	75
6.5	The Writers' Union	78
7	**Printing, paper and supplies**	**81**
7.1	Printing: administrative and economic position	81
7.2	Printer and publisher	83
7.3	Paper and other supplies	86
8	**The book trade**	**91**
8.1	The structure of the book trade	91
8.2	The economic position of the book trade	93
8.3	The book trade and the publishing-house	95
8.4	The consumer cooperative book trade network	99
8.5	The second-hand book trade	100
8.6	Book exports	100
9	**Special kinds of publication**	**102**
9.1	Types of exceptional treatment	102
9.2	Fiction	104
9.3	Political and social literature	105
9.4	Textbooks	108
9.5	Scientific and technical works	112
9.6	Children's books	113
9.7	Books for libraries	114

9.8	Works issued by organisations other than publishing-houses	115
9.9	Works translated from foreign languages	118
9.10	Forecasting demand and output for different types of publication	119
10	**Conclusions**	122
	Appendix 1. Authors' fee scales	127
	Appendix 2. All-union book retail prices	130
	Notes	137
	Select bibliography	155
	Index	159

TABLES

1. Departmental structure of the State Committee for Publishing 34
2. Effect of edition size on unit cost 64
3. Soviet demand and output forecasts for books and pamphlets, 1980 and 1990 120

Acknowledgments

This book has benefited from discussion with many people, but I should like to thank in particular Dr Philip Hanson, Mr Richard Newnham and Mr J. S. G. Simmons. I am also grateful to four institutions which gave me the opportunity to present lectures or seminars on aspects of the subject, and to take advantage of the comments made: St Antony's College, Oxford (Dr R. Kindersley); the Centre for Russian and East European Studies, University of Birmingham (Mr P. H. Kneen and Mrs J. J. Brine); the Harvard Ukrainian Research Institute (Mr Edward Kasinec); and the University of California, Berkeley (Dean Michael K. Buckland). The work is based on a thesis prepared for the University of Sheffield, and special thanks are due to my supervisors, Mr A. G. Waring and Mr F. S. Stych, and to my external examiner, Mr G. Barker. I am indebted to the Curators of the Bodleian Library and to Bodley's Librarian, Dr R. Shackleton, for the periods of study leave which have helped me so much in completing the undertaking.

Extracts from the work have appeared, or will shortly appear, in the book *Four studies in Soviet librarianship*, and in the journals *Library trends* and *Journal of documentation*. All are reproduced here with their respective publishers' permission.

I was able to visit Soviet publishing-houses, and other organisations connected with the publishing industry, in 1973 and 1975, and am happy to acknowledge the assistance of the British Council and the Academy of Sciences of the USSR. The staff of all the Soviet institutions concerned were most courteous and informative. Responsibility for the accurate representation of what I was told is, of course, entirely mine.

Finally, my greatest thanks go to my wife Anne and my parents for their unfailing support, for which the dedication of this book is an inadequate mark of gratitude.

G.P.M.W.

Wheatley, Oxford
1 May 1977

Glossary of specialised terms

Explanations are given below of specialised terms which occur frequently in the text or notes. Other such terms are defined briefly or translated where they first appear.

AUTHOR'S SHEET (*avtorskii list*). Unit measuring the amount of work written by an author, the basis for calculating his fee, and one measure of the work-load of a publishing-house's editorial staff. Equal to 40 000 typographical units of text, including spaces between words but excluding contents lists, illustrations, and other matter for which the author is not responsible. See also SHEET, PRINTED SHEET, PUBLISHER'S SHEET.

DECREE. Used to render Russian *ukaz* and *postanovlenie*. Both are rulings by the highest Soviet administrative and legislative organs. An *ukaz* is issued by the Presidium of the Supreme Soviet. A *postanovlenie* is issued by the Central Committee of the Communist Party, the Councils of Ministers of the USSR and the constituent republics, state committees, and a few other bodies.

EDITION SIZE (*tirazh*). The number of copies of a book printed in a single production operation. A single *tirazh* may be printed by more than one printing enterprise, but further identical copies ordered separately at a later date (within the time limit of the original contract with the author) are described as a *dopolnitel'nyi tirazh*, i.e. a second, or subsequent impression.

EDITOR (*redaktor*). A member of the staff of a publishing-house, or sometimes an outside consultant, responsible for one or more of the following: recommendations for the selection and commissioning of manuscripts; ideological, literary and factual examination and amendment of completed manuscripts; preparation of a manuscript for the printer, supervision of its progress in production, and monitoring of its reception by the public. A chief editor (*glavnyi redaktor*) supervises the entire editorial side of a publishing-house's operations. See also EDITORIAL OFFICE.

EDITORIAL OFFICE (*redaktsiya*). In a book publishing-house, a group of editors and ancillary staff, dealing with works in a particular area or with some other characteristic in common. In the charge of a 'head' (*zaveduyushchii redaktsiei*). See also EDITOR.

ORDER (*prikaz*). A ruling issued, approved or confirmed by the chairman of a state committee or by the minister of an all-union or republic ministry.

PRINTED (or PRINTER'S) SHEET (*pechatnyi list*). Unit measuring volume of book production and amount of paper consumed. As a 'natural' unit it may be one side of any standard paper format, but for comparative purposes is converted by coefficients to one side of a sheet 60 cm × 90 cm. See also SHEET, SHEET-COPY, PUBLISHER'S SHEET, AUTHOR'S SHEET.

PUBLISHER'S SHEET (*izdatel'skii* or *uchetno-izdatel'skii list*). Unit measuring amount of printing work. Equal to 40 000 typographical units, 700 lines of poetry or 3000 sq. cm of illustration. Includes spaces between words and all chapter headings, page numbers, contents lists, etc. See also SHEET, SHEET-COPY, PRINTED SHEET, AUTHOR'S SHEET.

REFEREE. See REVIEWER.

REISSUE (*pereizdanie*). Either the publication of a work in unaltered form after the expiry of the original contract period, or publication in altered form (i.e. a 'new edition') during or after that period.

REVIEWER (*retsenzent*). A distinction is made, following English usage, between a 'reviewer' and a 'referee', to both of whom the Russian *retsenzent* is applied. A referee writes a 'report', which is usually confidential, for the publisher or some other authority *before* publication of a work, whereas a reviewer writes a 'review', which is normally itself published, *after* the work appears in print.

SHEET (*list*). Sometimes translated as 'signature'. The usual Soviet unit of measurement for the physical extent of printed matter, measured in three ways for different purposes (see AUTHOR'S SHEET, PRINTED SHEET, PUBLISHER'S SHEET) and approximately equivalent to sixteen printed pages of an average-format book.

SHEET-COPY (*list-ottisk*). Either PUBLISHER'S SHEETS or PRINTED SHEETS may be the basis for this unit of measurement for book production, referred to respectively as 'publisher's sheet-copy' or 'printed sheet-copy', which equals the number of sheets in a book multiplied by the number of copies printed (the *tirazh*).

STATUTES. Used to render Russian *polozhenie* and *ustav*. Both are legal documents, confirmed by a DECREE or an ORDER, setting up an institution, organisation or enterprise and defining its rights, duties and basic structure.

THEMATIC PLAN (*tematicheskii plan, templan*). In its wider sense, any listing of specific publications or manuscripts, but more often applied to the publication plan (*plan vypuska literatury*) of works which a publisher intends to issue in a given year.

TITLE. Used in the text to denote books or pamphlets as bibliographically independent units. For example, the component volumes of a multi-volume work would not be regarded as separate titles, whereas a revised edition would rank as a different title from the original edition. To be distinguished from VOLUME.

VOLUME. Used to render the Russian *izdanie* in its specialised sense in Soviet publishing statistics, where it is defined as a typographically and physically distinct publication – often, and more accurately, called *pechatnaya edinitsa*. A ten-volume work would count as ten *izdaniya*, but as only one 'title' in the definition above.

Note on transliteration

The Cyrillic alphabet is transliterated and alphabetised according to the 'British' system of British Standard 2979:1958, with diacritics omitted.

References to journals and series

References to journals use the year of issue, followed by the issue number in brackets, when the journal carries no volume numbering. References to irregular numbered series give the volume number followed by the year of publication in brackets.

1

Introduction

1.1. *The study of Soviet book publishing*

In any international comparison, Soviet book publishing stands out on several counts. The first is scale: not only the scale of book copies published, but administrative scale. Soviet publishing, printing and book distribution, with a combined personnel of well over 300 000, are administered in many respects as a single undertaking. The organisational structures and techniques of control used in this administration are vastly more elaborate than those applied to Western publishing.

This great accretion of centralised administrative power is the product of persistent efforts by the Communist Party and the Soviet government to place the processes of book production and dissemination under a considerable degree of supervision – a degree which is, again, prominent in international comparisons. This commitment to effective supervision reflects the importance attributed to the role of publishing in a socialist society, and to the need for books produced under such supervision to be made readily accessible.

Most Western studies of Soviet publishing since the Second World War have devoted their chief attention to the restrictive control mechanisms (primarily censorship), to the effect of such restrictions on the variety of literature published, and to the phenomenon of *samizdat*, or the unauthorised private production and dissemination of material, to which the restrictions contributed.[1] Book publishing has been omitted, or dealt with very briefly, in Western works on the Soviet mass media as a whole.[2] Indeed, there seems to be a general reluctance in both East and West to accord book publishing the same rank among the mass media as broadcasting and the periodical press.[3] Accounts written by Western publishers who have visited the USSR reflect their principal concern with matters of contract negotiation and copyright protection, although the more extended reports also give valuable personal impressions, figures and miscellaneous information on other aspects of Soviet publishing.[4] The only work in a Western language to attempt a general

1

description of the Soviet publishing industry, based on Soviet sources, has been Boris I. Gorokhoff's *Publishing in the USSR* (Bloomington, 1959). Gorokhoff placed his chief emphasis on the formal organisational pattern of the industry and the effects of political influences on its operation. Economic considerations and matters of planning were not treated at length. However, the book's position as the standard work on the subject is being increasingly affected simply by the passage of time. Most of its statistical data is now twenty or more years old; and although the basic purposes and style of Soviet publishing administration have altered surprisingly little, many practices have been modified and many institutions recast and renamed.

The extensive journal and monographic literature on Soviet publishing which appears in the Soviet Union itself consists largely, as might be expected, of communication between practitioners. Soviet studies of publishing in the USSR have shown a strong inclination towards practical matters of organisation and economics.[5] More fundamental questions of national publishing policy which go beyond operational matters of this kind are debated in print only sporadically. For example, the difficulties of coordinating publishers' and printers' production plans are considered at length in the professional press, and the drawbacks of the present retail price structure have been pointed out on several occasions in recent years. By contrast the factors affecting the decision made in 1975 to increase the output of fiction have received a very limited airing, and the USSR's adherence to the Universal Copyright Convention in 1973 was preceded by no published discussion whatever.

1.2. *Soviet publishing policy and the present work*

This book is a study of contemporary publishing policy in the Soviet Union, as applied to non-periodical publications. The term 'policy' is open to a variety of interpretations, but is used here to characterise those decisions and actions lying within an organisation's competence which are regarded as most important to its overall objectives.[6] This definition requires two comments. Firstly, my concern is with decisions *and* actions, not with decisions or 'decision-making' exclusively. I have taken the study of the policy-making process as covering the identification of issues important to the organisations concerned; examination of debates and opinions expressed on the issues; and analysis of action taken or avoided in respect of those issues.[7] These three procedures taken together will sometimes furnish grounds for hypotheses about 'decision-making'; but, as the previous section has already suggested, Soviet sources do not supply direct evidence of the detailed circumstances surrounding significant decisions in publishing administration, except occasionally at the level of the individual publishing-house.

Secondly, I have treated 'policy' as being the *most important* decisions and actions open to an organisation. This requires a consideration of the priorities and imperatives observed by each body (ill-perceived or conflicting though they will be on occasions), and a recognition of the fact that organisations at different levels, or with different interests in the publishing process, will often have different priorities, and will view differing types of decision and action as 'policy'. For example, a Soviet publishing-house may have a 'policy' of paying high (or low) fees to its authors, but the upper and lower limits of the fee scales themselves are a matter of 'policy' for the State Committee for Publishing, in consultation with other government departments, the Writers' Union and probably the Department of Propaganda of the Communist Party's Central Committee.

The book begins with an account (chapter 2) of the political and social significance and the economic status attributed by Soviet opinion to book publishing, in order to indicate some of the general assumptions and expectations to which book publishing policy is subject. This is followed by treatments of the organisations and groups which are the most authoritative and influential parties to publishing policy: the Communist Party (chapter 3); central government organs, especially the State Committee for Publishing (chapter 4); publishing-houses (chapter 5); authors (chapter 6); the printing and paper industries (chapter 7); the book trade (chapter 8); and the readership of different kinds of publication (chapter 9). The authority or influence of each body in policy-making is assessed with reference to the scope and nature of its powers and obligations (whether formal or informal); the kinds of issue which face it; the ways in which it exercises its powers and meets its obligations in practice, and the priorities and imperatives which it observes in so doing. Chapter 10 presents conclusions. Appendix 1 shows the scales for authors' fees in force since 1975 in one of the union republics, the Russian Soviet Federal Socialist Republic (RSFSR), and appendix 2 the all-union retail price-list for books, introduced in 1972. Neither of these documents has previously appeared in English.

The intention of this approach is to go beyond a simple organisational description of how Soviet publishing 'works', by showing something of the effect on each other of – on the one hand – the peculiarities and limitations characteristic of book publishing as a medium and as an industry, and – on the other hand – contemporary Soviet institutions and accepted Soviet attitudes. A second intention is to illustrate the impact of all the foregoing on books now being published in the Soviet Union, from the content of a single work to the composition of Soviet book production as a whole.

Some limitations in scope should be noted. This is primarily an analysis of contemporary practice in an industry which has changed comparatively little in its formal organisation and relations with the rest of Soviet society since the establishment of the State Committee for the Press in 1963. For this reason events in the history of Soviet book publishing are recounted only where they are felt to be very specifically relevant to its present situation. Secondly, this is not a comparative study of Soviet and Western publishing, although comparisons with publishing outside the USSR have been made on occasion to point up certain contrasts. Thirdly, I have not treated systematically the differences in publishing practice as applied to the various Soviet republics, nationalities or languages; further research in this direction would be rewarding. Finally, I have tried to give the system of formal censorship due significance, and have also dealt with other kinds of scrutiny applied to books; but I have devoted much more space to those matters of policy which bear on the production of over 80 000 different books and pamphlets a year, than to those which prevent or inhibit the appearance of an unknown number of others.

1.3. *Materials used*

Formal statements of policy on publishing affairs, which occur most frequently in Central Committee decrees, have been drawn upon extensively; and the large and varied corpus of Party- and government-approved regulations for the administration of the publishing industry has been examined in detail, in the belief that the instructions which specify and alter the powers of government agencies and publishing enterprises, and which lay down the manner in which they conduct their affairs, compose a framework for their operations which expresses policy on many aspects of book publishing. In dealing with the position of the author in Soviet publishing, the civil legislation and accompanying commentaries on authors' rights have been examined with the same intention.

For Soviet comment on official statements and directives, and for accounts throwing light on the manner in which the book publishing system functions in practice, specialised monographs, journals and some newspaper articles have been used – particularly those journals produced by the publishing, printing and bookselling sector for its own staff. The most informative of these, *Izdatel'skoe delo. Referativnaya informatsiya*, is not commercially available in Western countries.[8] Personal visits to Soviet publishing-houses and other organisations connected with book publishing, in July 1973 and March 1975, made it possible to clarify many points of detail and to gauge, from interviews with senior staff, something of the relative importance which they attached to factors affecting planning processes and economic management. Some use has also been made of accounts published outside the USSR by visiting Western publishers and by individuals with personal experience of Soviet publishing practice.

Soviet publishing statistics, where they are quoted, are accompanied whenever appropriate by a note on definitions used and discrepancies detected. This caution is dictated by an admitted lack of uniformity (at least until a revised method of compilation was adopted in 1974) between statistics recorded by the All-Union Book Chamber and the figures reported by publishing-houses to their own superior authorities.[9]

2

The political and economic view of Soviet publishing

The organisations and groups which play a part in Soviet book publishing do so against a background of authoritatively accepted opinion about the position and purposes of book publishing in a socialist society. The views expressed are by no means unanimous in their emphasis. The principles of Party spirit (*partiinost'*), closeness to the people (*narodnost'*), and direction by Party and government are not placed in question;[1] but other matters quite fundamental to the ideological function and economic status of book publishing are under active debate – although a dominant or more deeply established view is often discernible. This chapter examines some of the most important prevailing assumptions and disputes about publishing as an act of industrial production; about demand and pricing; subsidy and profit; quality, effectiveness and optimality; and the power of the reader.

2.1. *Publishing as production*

There is general acceptance in the USSR that publishing, like the other mass media, is in some sense a cultural, and more specifically an ideological activity. The State Committee for Publishing, Printing and the Book Trade of the USSR Council of Ministers is often classified as an organ of cultural organisation, alongside the Ministry of Culture, the State Committee for Television and Radio, the State Committee for Cinematography, and the Committee for Physical Culture and Sport. To a much greater degree than the other mass media, however, Soviet publishing depends on a considerable industrial capacity to fulfil its cultural and ideological purposes: over 83 000 book and pamphlet volumes in nearly 1.7 thousand million copies were issued in 1975.[2] The question of publishing's place in the Marxist analysis of production relations continues to arouse controversy which throws some interesting light on Soviet views of the function of publishing, despite the restricted premises on which the argument is conducted.

Marx and Engels are credited with 'having first discovered the

6

class nature of the book' (which appears to mean essentially that the purposes of book publishing may be as various as the purposes of any other form of communication), and with having demonstrated the bourgeois transformation of the book into a commodity (*tovar*).[3] It is common ground, among modern Soviet commentators on the subject, that a book, though a commodity, is a special kind of commodity; and secondly, that its status in a socialist society is qualitatively different from its status under capitalism. It is claimed that a Soviet author does not 'sell' a 'product', as an author would to a capitalist publisher, because the fee he receives is for the use of his work in the interests of all society, whereas the capitalist publishing-house has the two aims of maximum profit and of serving the interests of bourgeois society.[4] (Potential clashes of interest between these two imputed aims have not, so far as I know, been further examined.) An excessively profit-orientated approach to publishing, at the expense of what are regarded as the interests of a socialist society, is often warned against; and the admonition has been made that to inflate a publishing-house's profits by such devices as increasing the issue of books in heavy demand, or simplifying the design of a work, is to satisfy 'commercial interests on an unhealthy basis'.[5]

In a socialist society, it is maintained in one line of argument, the value of a book, and hence of a publishing-house's production, is determined basically by its ideological content.[6] Demand and profitability cannot be allowed to be the sole guides in the matter of which books to publish, otherwise highly specialised works and books in minority languages (to quote two common examples) would never appear. Due to the peculiar nature of the value of its products, this argument continues, publishing is a branch of 'non-material production' (*nematerial'noe proizvodstvo*), and its economics cannot be compared directly with those of manufacturing industry. The view expressed frequently from the late 1920s up to the early 1940s, that publishing was simply another branch of industry, to which industrial terms could be automatically applied, is attacked as a vulgarisation which disregards the ideological function of published matter.[7]

A divergent approach by L. S. Glyazer (who produced the first mathematical model of publishing economics to appear in the USSR, in 1969) took the line that publishing, like broadcasting and the cinema, is 'mental production' (*dukhovnoe proizvodstvo*), but that it *is* permissible to discuss the economics of mental production using the same terms as those applied to material production, and that these terms need not have the 'purely conventional significance' usually attributed to them in evaluating ideological work.[8]

A different argument has been that a book also has a value determined by the expenditure on its production, since production cost is one of the elements (though not the only one) in a book's retail price; and that, for this reason, although the book is an ideological commodity and the chief aim of publishing a work is to achieve a desired social impact, nevertheless a publishing-house functions in both the material and the non-material spheres of production.[9] A refinement of this view (perhaps an over-refinement) is that the sale for money of books whose purpose is ideological shows the dialectical relationship between ideology and economics in publishing.[10]

The printing industry is said to be indisputably a branch of material production, and one which is intended to satisfy mental needs in the same way as industries making television sets or musical instruments;[11] but the place assigned to publishing remains unclear. Publishing-houses are regarded as production organisations, mostly operating on *khozraschet* (i.e. as separate accounting units) and subject to the decree 'On the socialist state enterprise' – all of which are characteristics of enterprises in other sectors of Soviet industry; but the State Planning Committee (Gosplan) classifies the planning of publishing as a branch of cultural planning, like the planning of clubs, libraries and broadcasting, and handles publishing through its Department of Culture and Education, separating it from the planning of printing, which is classed as an industry.[12]

The idea of the book as a 'direct force in production', which can contribute measurable improvements to the country's economic performance, has been aired by several Soviet writers. One has gone so far as to estimate savings achieved in the construction industry through the use of certain works on improved organisation,[13] and others have calculated that engineering plants could gain 8450 roubles per year by improved performance from each machine-tool to which they applied the advice in the book *Adaptivnoe upravlenie stankami* (*Adaptive control of machine-tools*, published by Mashinostroenie in 1973).[14] One scholar has taken this thinking to the point of suggesting that a loss-making book should have its losses made good by a deduction from the profits of the industry in whose interests it was published.[15] The difficulty in applying such calculations to the great majority of books is obvious; but this view of the book (or of some books) as having a determinable effect on the economy remains as one argument among others used to justify the publication of loss-making works.

2.2. *Demand and pricing policy*

The place of reader demand in book publishing has received equivocal treatment in the USSR. It has been generally agreed, as a corollary of the arguments already summarised, that undifferentiated satisfaction of 'raw' demand, as expressed in pre-publication orders and queues in bookshops, is not the primary aim of socialist publishing. Concern is nevertheless expressed over the shortage of books in certain fields – at present particularly fiction and children's books – and over the importance of ensuring the 'right' proportion of each type of book in the total output. It was claimed in 1975, by a deputy chairman of the State Committee for Publishing of the Ukrainian SSR, that supply is further behind demand in publishing than in any other sphere of production aimed at satisfying mental needs.[16]

Some Soviet commentators have applied to publishing the distinction between 'demand' (*spros*) and 'need' (*potrebnost'*), arguing that publishing should be guided by needs, rather than by demand and (concomitantly) profit. A theme which frequently accompanies this suggestion is that the tastes of the Soviet people must be 'formed', a process in which publishers are said to have an important role.[17] Demand, in other words, must be educated to become more closely identical with authoritatively defined needs; and the book trade has on occasion been accused of placing over-large orders for 'time-honoured' works which presumably reflect uneducated demand. Glyazer has maintained, however, that readers' *needs* cannot be accurately measured for the purposes of economic decisions, whereas their demand *can* be measured, and should be the basis for determining a pricing structure and fixing rational volumes of production for different types of literature.[18]

The approved view of retail pricing policy in Soviet publishing is far removed from that of Glyazer, who appears, in fact, to be advocating that prices should reflect the state of the market and should if necessary be adjusted to alter the demand pattern. The existing price system is regarded by its supporters as an important means of giving effect to a book's ideological function, by ensuring that books intended to be widely accessible bear low prices, even though this may lead to some titles, and even entire publishing-houses, making a loss and requiring a subsidy. This policy claims consciously to deny itself the use of higher prices either as a means of limiting demand or as a stimulus to publishers' economic performance.[19]

Book retail prices were set separately by each publishing-house until 1952, since when a succession of standard national price-lists has been in force, using the principle of so many kopeks per publisher's sheet. (A sheet is roughly equal to sixteen printed pages.) Although the price-lists have given some recognition to quality of paper and binding, and to the presence of illustrations or colour printing, their major principle of differentiation, which has increased in detail over the years, is by subject-matter. The price-list now in force (introduced in 1972, amended in 1977, and extracts from which are shown in appendix 2) enumerates 191 different types of book and pamphlet according to their subject and intended readership, compared with 129 in the superseded price-list of 1965. The principles on which the price-lists are drawn up have never been stated in detail. Production costs for each type of literature are only one consideration; but it is accepted that, for most types of book, the retail price (less the wholesale discount) should enable the publisher to cover his production costs and make a profit. The production cost element in retail prices is based on average costs and edition sizes for each of the types of work in the price-list.[20] Provision is made for works published in small editions to be priced at up to 15k. per sheet to avoid a loss. The basic range of prices is between 2k. and 10k. per sheet, with school textbooks as low as 1k. per sheet. (A kopek – one-hundredth of a rouble – was worth about 0.8 pence or 1.4 cents at the 1977 official rate of exchange.) Books requiring especially complex printing work may be given a price founded directly on production costs.[21]

These exceptional cases apart, however, book retail pricing is not an integral part of the annual and longer-term economic planning cycles in the publishing industry. Prices are not automatically altered to take account of rises in printing and paper costs, although charges for printing and paper have formed an increasing proportion of publishers' production costs, rising from 46.3 per cent in 1947 to 73.3 per cent in 1967 in a selection of central publishing-houses.[22] The bulk of prices in the original 1972 list were identical with those laid down in the 1965 list, insofar as direct comparisons are possible, although the extra costs of publishing translations were more generously allowed for, and higher prices were introduced for illustrated works of superior quality. Substantial amendments to the 1972 price-list were, however, introduced in 1977. They raised prices (in many cases doubling, and occasionally even tripling them) for fiction, encyclopedias, dictionaries, books on domestic pursuits and hobbies, and small-edition scholarly works. Higher charges for printing and paper, as well as increases in authors' fees, were on this occasion given as the reason.[23] Nevertheless, it may well be no coincidence that all these types of literature (except scholarly works) are among those suffering the heaviest unsatisfied demand; and an attempt to reduce that demand by massive price increases would hardly be surprising.

Despite such evidence of occasional price alterations to affect the market, it seems probable that production costs are the most important factor in price-setting, but that political, or purely traditional, views on low book prices are allowed to be an overriding consideration in the case of certain types of publication only. This frequently reiterated general principle, that the price should not hamper a book's circulation among the readers for whom it is intended, appears most prominently in the pricing of school textbooks and of works in minority languages.

2.3. *Profits and subsidies*

As we have already seen, profit and loss are not admitted to be overriding considerations in Soviet publishing. Efficient economic performance by publishing-houses is frequently stressed, however, and profitability is one of the yardsticks used to assess it. Profitability has received increased emphasis since the publishing industry began its transfer to the new planning and incentive system at the end of the 1960s. A decree of the Communist Party's Central Committee in 1970 on improving the profitability of book publishing noted that the state budget was currently receiving profits of 120 million roubles annually from book and journal publishing, but that subsidies to publishing-houses, at that time running at over nine million roubles annually, were unacceptably high.[24] (Disguised subsidies in the form of cheap capital have less impact in publishing than in most Soviet industries, since publishers' capital requirements are relatively low.) However, in 1976, forty-one publishing-houses in the State Committee's system (over a quarter of the total, but accounting for only 10 per cent of production) were still running on

a planned-loss basis, and the amount of such losses was still about
nine million roubles a year. Many were said to be houses specialising in low-priced textbooks, and a large number were in the peripheral republics. Eight of the fifteen union republic publishing
administrations reported losses from publishing in 1975.[25] Many of
the fifty-odd publishing-houses not directly subordinated to the
State Committee's system probably also make a loss.

Books, like most other forms of printed matter except calendars,
picture reproductions and postcards, are not subject to turnover tax
at either the printing or publishing stage; but the deduction of a
large part of an enterprise's profits to the state budget is, of course,
a different form of taxation, and publishing-houses are subject to
this on the same footing as other enterprises if their profits are
substantial enough to warrant it. The state can, of course, deduct
'surplus' profit at any figure it thinks fit from a publishing-house or
any other enterprise; so the fact that a publishing-house escapes
turnover tax does not necessarily (and in fact does not) mean that it
can retain more of its profits than an enterprise subject to that tax.
Publishing-houses and printing enterprises of union subordination
in the system of the State Committee for Publishing passed on to
the state 395 million roubles out of the 514 million roubles profit
which they secured between 1971 and 1973 – that is, 76.8 per cent.[26]

The enhanced role given to profit under the economic reform
has been accompanied in the publishing industry by attempts to
make profit act as an incentive for improving a book's quality and
social impact, and for ensuring that titles in a publishing-house's
annual plan are issued on schedule. So far, however, it has not
proved possible to make profit other than directly dependent upon
production costs, overheads and payments to the state budget on the
one hand, and upon income from sales on the other. Quality, as
distinct from saleability, and adherence to the annual publishing
plan, have had to be made simply conditions for the award of full
bonuses to the publishing-house staff.

The regime of *khozraschet*, under which an enterprise functions
as a separate accounting unit with fixed responsibility for the use of
resources allocated to it, is established in the Soviet publishing
industry in the sense that nearly all publishing-houses proper are
described as being 'on *khozraschet*'. The initial decision to place
publishers on *khozraschet* was taken as early as November 1921
under the New Economic Policy, superseding the qualified commitment to the distribution of some books at below cost price which

had been foreshadowed in the Decree on the State Publishing-House of December 1917.[27] The principle according to which enterprises on *khozraschet* are obliged to cover their expenditure from their revenue is not consistently observed in publishing, although the view has been put that 'full *khozraschet*' in publishing should imply that not only the publishing-house but every one of its products – that is, each title – is covering its costs.[28] In practice, publishing-houses making a planned loss are also said to operate on *khozraschet*, although only 'in a juridical sense'.[29]

2.4. *Quality, effectiveness and optimality*

Although the importance of profits as an indicator in plan fulfilment has been enhanced in recent years, the two most important yardsticks by which fulfilment is judged remain the annual plan of titles to be issued and the total volume of output in printed sheet-copies. It has been pointed out that none of the many indicators applied to the planning and analysis of publishing work enables any 'reliable' assessment before publication of the quality of a book's contents. Qualitative criteria, by which a publishing-house's superior organ could assess the ideological, scientific or literary worth of the house's output, are regarded as highly desirable, but have yet to emerge in any trustworthy form. The suggestion has been made that, instead of measuring output in printed sheet-copies, i.e. the number of single sheets printed, which only shows the amount of paper used, the unit of a publisher's sheet-copy should be employed, which would measure the amount of text and illustrations.[30]

Another proposal has been that a 'coefficient of effectiveness' should be calculated for each title, putting a value on its importance and the standard of its treatment, and that this value should be incorporated into planning indicators, as well as into authors' fees and book prices.[31] The fact that this elaborate superstructure turns out to rest ultimately on a personal, even if 'expert' opinion of each work, points up the difficulty of finding a consistent measure for some notional 'worth' of a book which does not depend on either volume of demand or sales revenue. The Soviet practice of paying authors primarily according to the length of their work, rather than according to sales or 'quality' alone, probably survives because of the same difficulty. The most recent attempt at establishing criteria for the 'effectiveness' of publishing admits to two assumptions: that a publishing-house's annual publication plan fully expresses social needs, and that demand is forecast correctly.[32] That the quest for such criteria continues in the USSR suggests a persisting desire to find some means of judging a work definitively before it is entrusted to the possibly unreliable verdict of the reading public.

Some had hoped to see 'optimal' planning methods become widespread in the publishing, printing and bookselling sector as a result of the economic reform. Optimal planning was canvassed as a procedure which would use mathematical methods to allow the choice of the most effective use of economic resources in achieving the planners' intentions; but the application of these methods has in fact been as limited in the field of publishing as in most other sectors of Soviet industry.[33] All the optimal planning procedures discussed for publishing since the economic reform began take as a starting-point the publishing-house's finalised annual publication plan: that is, optimal planning is assumed to begin only in the choice of subordinate alternatives, *after* the most significant decisions have been taken on which titles will be issued, how much paper and printing capacity will be allocated to the publisher, and what his output target will be.[34] The issue of 'demand' versus 'need' is thus avoided in discussions of optimality in publishing. Although publishing-houses retain a measure of discretion in their choice of manuscripts (subject to their superior organs' approval), the allocation of materials and production facilities is effectively out of their hands; and since publishers cannot influence demand through a flexible pricing system, they are reduced to manipulating the edition size (*tirazh*) of each book title, which is the only important planning variable remaining to a considerable degree under their own control, in order to achieve maximum profits from 'optimum' edition sizes.

The idea of 'optimality' recently appeared in a different context when the State Committee for Publishing began studies to establish what are described as the 'optimal proportions' of different types of publication and different subjects in the total output of printed matter. These proportions are now being planned at all-union and republic level more systematically than before. At least one republic's publishing administration (that of the RSFSR) has explicitly concluded that it must choose between itself compiling a single plan for the issue of every title in the republic, and regulating publishing-houses' own plans in order to achieve the most desirable proportions.[35] It has chosen the latter course; presumably the former would remove the fundamental *raison d'être* of the publishing-houses themselves. The criteria for this kind of optimality have not been stated, but publication plans for 1976–80, which are said to express 'optimal' judgments, suggest that the degree of unsatisfied reader demand has strongly influenced the way in which existing proportions are to be altered.

One of the most significant recent steps has been the reversal of the decision, taken in the mid-1960s, to give priority to expanding production of journals and newspapers at the expense of books because periodicals were allegedly more efficient (*operativnyi*) as sources of information.[36] The precise evidence which resulted in quantitative restrictions being removed from periodical subscriptions in 1965, and which effectively resulted in the entire growth in paper supplies during the second half of the 1960s being devoted to increasing the number of copies of periodicals issued, has not been made public. The effects of the decision are nevertheless indicated by the statistics. Between 1960 and 1970, the annual *tirazh* of journals increased by 246 per cent, of newspapers by 108 per cent, and of books by only 6 per cent.[37] (The total value of retail sales of *printed matter* as a whole has remained in much the same proportion to the total value of non-food sales in the Soviet retail trade for at least thirty-five years: 2.83 per cent in 1940, 2.24 per cent in 1960, 2.51 per cent in 1970 and 2.38 per cent in 1975.)[38]

During the period 1975–80, however, the State Committee for Publishing intends to devote the entire planned increase in its paper supplies to raising the output of fiction, and is adopting several other measures to increase the amount of children's books, textbooks and reference works at the expense of categories of publication in less demand.[39] This action has not so far been accompanied by any public discussion of the reasons why the supply of these types of book, which has long been behind demand, should be permitted such a substantial improvement at this particular juncture. The surmise seems justified that the degree of under-fulfilment of orders for such works became so blatant and so widely criticised (see chapter 9) that pressure from publishers, and more indirectly from readers, in this instance convinced the Central Committee's Department of Propaganda and the State Committee for Publishing that under-supply had gone far enough.

2.5. *The power of the reader*

It appears to be the case that certain powerful and pervasive convictions are present among senior policy-makers in the Soviet publishing administration, and that it is easier for policy decisions to follow or express these convictions than to run counter to them. Among such convictions are: that publishing should be strictly regulated by the Party and the state; that it should reflect the views of Party and state about what should be read; and that Soviet citizens should be encouraged by low prices to read the books produced under this supervision. These convictions are reflected in the importance attached to reading as a factor in forming the individual's social consciousness, and a considerable amount of work has been done in the Soviet Union on a variety of questions touching upon the sociology of the book and the psychology of reading.[40] Some of it has been criticised for failing to study ways of influencing the individual's choice and pattern of reading; and it has been remarked that Soviet cultural administration should take account of an alleged fall in 'social forms of cultural consumption' in favour of 'individual' forms of such consumption, which – like reading – are domestic and passive in character, and harder to place under social supervision (*kontrol'*).[41]

Rather ironically, some of this research into reading and the use of books in contemporary Soviet society appears to have had a powerful influence on publishing policy by providing, for the first time, well-grounded and voluminous evidence of the difficulties which so many readers experience in gaining access to the books they want. The widest discussion so far has been aroused by a study of the book and reading in small towns, undertaken by the Lenin Library between 1969 and 1971.[42] The most pressing of its conclusions was generally taken to be that the growth of readers' requirements was 'coming into contradiction with' opportunities for meeting those requirements, particularly in the case of readers not living in the larger cities. The frequency with which that work's figures and conclusions have subsequently been quoted by senior individuals in Soviet publishing circles when speaking of the need for improved book supplies, suggests that it carried weight in the adoption of the measures taken in 1975 to economise in the use of paper and alter the composition of book production.

At the same time, a separate force exists outside the policy-making procedures of the Party, the State Committee for Publishing and the publishing-houses, which exercises a considerable influence on their decisions. This consists of the potential purchasers and potential readers – two overlapping but not identical groups. The influence exerted by these groups stems from the fact that the very nature of publishing, in the USSR as in the West, requires the maximum amount of output to be bought (leaving aside unpriced publications, which even in the USSR are not widespread).[43] As the director of the Lenin Library has observed, a book is a *social* phenomenon: if it remains unread, it is merely a packet of paper.[44] Although certain groups of reader are more or less compelled to acquire certain types of book (students following a particular course, say, or an enterprise needing instructions to maintain equipment), a great deal of published matter must rely to some degree on its intrinsic merits to attract the purchaser to buy and the reader to read, although of course a variety of external constraints and incentives can also be applied. The fact that paper shortages and book pricing policies have combined to make Soviet book publishing at present a sellers' market does not alter the fact that a market relationship exists. The millions of individual decisions to buy or not to buy collectively apply a separate range of constraints and incentives on the publishing industry and its administrators, to which is added the more direct stimulus that publishers are liable to booksellers for half the value of books remaining unsold in the bookshops (see 8.3).

An increasing awareness of pressure from this direction is shown by the growing attention being paid in the USSR to the study and forecasting of reader demand: by departments of the State Committees for Publishing at all-union and republic level, and by the All-Union Book Chamber, the Moscow Polygraphic Institute and other bodies. This forecasting (some prognoses of which are discussed in 9.10) is explicitly concerned with demand, rather than with any officially defined 'needs', which suggests that Soviet 'reader power' is beginning to prove a partial counterpoise to administrative rulings on what ought to be read.

3

The Communist Party

Having noted in the previous chapter the 'leading role' which is attributed to the Communist Party (CPSU) in publishing, as in other matters, we review in this chapter the institutions and methods through which the Party participates in book publishing policy: the apparatus of the Central Committee and its Secretariat; the powers of the Party at the level of the individual publishing-house, and in the printing industry and the book trade; the Party as a publisher in its own right; and the general character of the Party's exercise of its authority.

3.1. *The Central Committee and the Department of Propaganda*

Party intervention at the highest level, in the name of the Politburo and the Central Committee, comes most usually in the form of Central Committee decrees on a wide variety of topics, both general and highly specific; and less frequently by means of individual leaders' pronouncements on which the publishing industry is expected to take action. Most of the decrees are likely to originate in proposals from the Secretariat of the Central Committee, and are believed to be issued in most instances on the authority of the Secretariat's own standing executive apparatus, without the need for ratification by the Central Committee itself.[1] The Secretariat's Department of Propaganda (until 1966 the Department of Agitation and Propaganda) maintains standing contact with the State Committee for Publishing, Printing and the Book Trade, the government organ which administers the sector as a whole. The Department of Propaganda is the highest Party agency with a direct and constant responsibility for publishing affairs, as well as for the press, radio and television, and the State Committee for Publishing is subject to its instructions and guidance.[2]

Besides initiating action on situations in publishing which require Central Committee decrees or less formal measures, and checking on the response to such action, the Department of Propaganda directly controls the most senior staff appointments in the publishing industry by means of its 'second category' *nomenklatura* list;[3] and through local and primary Party organisations it transmits directives, receives reports and influences staffing down to the level of the individual publishing-house. The union and republic state committees for publishing, like other state administrative bodies, have their own internal apparatus of Party organs at central and local level, which are required to watch over the fulfilment of Party and government directives and the observance of laws. The Party is also strongly represented on the Publishing Council of the union State Committee for Publishing.

The Central Committee's decrees establish practice on some of the most fundamental issues in Soviet publishing, as well as on many that are less fundamental, and often charge Party bodies with supervising their implementation. For example, a decree of 1970 affirmed the power of the Department of Propaganda to approve or refuse the granting to any organisation of the right to issue printed matter.[4] (In the USSR, this is a right which must be explicitly conferred, and one which is in practice never conferred on individuals.) The state committees' part in the granting of publishing rights remains simply the consideration of proposals for such grants put to them for approval. An earlier Central Committee decree instructed Glavlit, the main censorship organ, to inform Party organs of any cases it detected of institutions issuing their own publications without permission.[5]

The establishment of a new publishing-house, journal or newspaper is also a matter for decision by the Central Committee, while the State Committee for Publishing, to which most publishing-houses are formally subordinated, only has the power to express an opinion on such proposals.[6] The major internal reorganisation of a publishing-house, or modification of its area of specialisation, may also be the subject of Party instructions. It was, for example, a Central Committee decree which created two separate houses out of the former Sovetskii Khudozhnik enterprise in 1968, laid down their respective fields of activity, and specified to which organs they should be subordinated.[7] Central committees of the republic Parties intervene in similar matters affecting publishers at their own level, as when the Central Committee of the Belorussian Communist Party instructed that republic's State Committee for Publishing to create a new editorial office in the Belarus' house to deal with literature on the fine arts.[8]

Economic and planning policies in publishing at all-union level are likewise the subject of Central Committee decrees. One such, in 1970, expressed disquiet at the amount of money needed to subsidise loss-making publishers, and instructed the (then) Committee for the Press, the Ministry of Finance and the State Committee for Prices to prepare an improved retail pricing scheme for books, for the Central Committee's approval.[9] Another decree in the same year regulated in considerable detail the organisation of publishing activities by ministries, departments and other organisations which were not themselves publishing-houses. Approval for changes in the scales of authors' fees laid down by the Council of Ministers of the RSFSR has also to be given by the CPSU Central Committee.[10]

The Party's concern with the content and ideological orientation of books is reflected in numerous decrees, some affecting whole categories of literature, others only single works. The Central Committee's now-defunct Ideological Commission had the task of studying draft publication plans for literature in fields felt to be of particular importance, and it is believed that all publishers' plans are now scanned in draft by staff of the Department of Propaganda.[11] It is known that equivalent departments of the republic Parties' central committees also review and amend local publishers' plans.[12]

As examples of intervention over particular types of literature, a wide range of specific measures was laid down in 1967 for improving the effectiveness of socio-political literature, including improved fee scales and closer guidance by Party authorities.[13] In 1969, another decree required a radical improvement in the quality and supply of children's books;[14] and in 1972 a decree on literary and artistic criticism emphasised the importance of securing Party involvement in critical writing.[15]

'Instructional meetings' are believed to be held at two-weekly intervals by the Department of Propaganda for leading staff of the mass media, including the main publishing-houses, to transmit up-to-date information on current Party policy.[16] The Central Committee also arranges occasional larger conferences for such staff at which more fundamental directives (*ukazaniya*) are apparently laid down or restated.[17]

The pronouncements of higher Party leaders, expressed by means other than Central Committee decrees, may also bring about changes in the content of publications. In 1971 the director of the Ekonomika publishing-house gave as an example Soviet textbooks on political economy. These had formerly stated that Soviet society possessed two classes (workers and peasants), and that possible contradictions between them could be resolved through the guidance of the Party. However, L. I. Brezhnev had stated at the 24th Party Congress that socialist construction had produced in the Soviet people a new historical community, in which the Party ensured the harmony of the classes' interests. This rather subtle change in nuance was 'a new position and a new step in development', which should henceforth be incorporated into the textbooks.[18]

Individual works, where they are deemed to be of particular ideological or political significance, may be ruled upon by the highest Party organs. It was Central Committee decrees which initiated preparation of the third edition of the *Bol'shaya sovetskaya entsiklopediya* (*Great Soviet encyclopedia*) and of the twelve-volume *Istoriya vtoroi mirovoi voiny 1939–1945gg.* (*History of the Second World War 1939–1945*), and which severely censured those responsible for the sixty-fifth volume of the series *Literaturnoe nasledstvo*, entitled *Novoe o Mayakovskom* (*New materials on Mayakovskii*), which was described as publishing documents on Mayakovskii of an intimate and personal character which allowed it to be used for anti-Soviet purposes.[19]

The Central Committee, primarily through its Department of Propaganda, maintains direct contact with other bodies, besides the State Committee for Publishing, which exert considerable influence on the selection, content and availability of publications. Perhaps the most significant of these is Glavlit, the main censorship organ. Until August 1966 Glavlit was formally subordinated to the Committee for the Press. It was then placed directly under the USSR Council of Ministers;[20] but there is evidence that, in practice, important matters relating to censorship are decided by the Department of Propaganda, to whom Glavlit submits reports on what it regards as dubious material. A former Soviet journal editor has recounted how a report from Glavlit, claiming that the journal *Znanie-sila* was publishing science fiction stories containing political allusions, resulted in a reprimand to the journal from the Department of Propaganda.[21] The operation of the censorship is treated further in 5.9.

The network of Peoples' Control agencies, which enable the public to participate in identifying cases of mismanagement and maladministration, is itself firmly supervised by the Party, and acts in effect as another arm of Party control. At the highest level, the USSR Committee for Peoples' Control in 1974 criticised the printing subsector of the State Committee for Publishing for uneconomic practices. Although no specific remedies were imposed, the State Committee was moved to issue a general instruction on improving performance, and to draw attention to its proposed reorganisation of the printing industry.[22]

The Central Committee is believed also to have a decisive voice in the actions of the Writers' Union of the USSR through the latter's Secretariat and Party organisation (described further in 6.5), on such questions as whether to recommend publication of controversial literary manuscripts; and there is similar Party influence in the writers' unions of the republics. The recently established mass organisation to encourage an interest in books, the All-Union Voluntary Association of Book-Lovers, has received close attention from the Central Committee's Secretariat since its inception, and even has the head of Glavlit, P. K. Romanov, as a member of its central executive.[23]

3.2. *The Party in the publishing-house*

Seen from the viewpoint of the publishing-house, Party policy will impinge on it from several different points: as instructions from the Central Committee and consultations with its Department of Propaganda, either directly or through the State Committee for Publishing; through local Party organs (in the case of provincial publishing-houses); through Party representatives on the house's editorial council; and through the constant interaction between the management and the house's own organisation of Party members. Some of the managing and editorial staff are, besides, likely to have received training in Party-supervised establishments such as the Higher Party School or the Academy of Social Sciences. One-month courses on Party policy as applied to publishing have been introduced at the Higher Party School, and are attended by many senior staff, including publishing-house directors.[24] Some staff may have been placed in the house on the direct instructions of the Party authorities, to 'strengthen' its work;[25] and the appointment to, and removal from, all posts carrying much more than clerical responsibilities will in any case require Party approval at some level. Few staff are likely to reach senior posts within the publishing-house (except perhaps in the technical and design departments) without becoming Party or Komsomol members. It was reported, for instance, in 1975 that the majority of departmental and editorial office heads in Moldavian publishing-houses were Party members.[26]

A single house's editorial policy may be the subject of a Central Committee ruling, as when the Publishing-House for Foreign Literature was ordered in 1959 to make omissions and annotations where necessary in issuing works by bourgeois authors on philosophy, history, law, diplomacy and economics.[27] (This order would now be incompatible with the Soviet Union's commitments under the Universal Copyright Convention.) Where a publisher decides to send a manuscript to an outside referee, the contract between the parties stipulates that the referee's report must state the extent to which the manuscript meets the ideological requirements of the Party.

Important Party events and campaigns can deeply affect a publishing-house's planning and output, and lead to drastic modification of its usual procedures. It is not surprising that, in houses specialising in political literature, unsolicited manuscripts contribute only a small proportion of the titles issued, while the majority of books in the annual plan consist of works commissioned by the house on the basis of a study of Party documents and contact with Party officials.[28] In addition to consulting Party representatives in the preparation of its plans, a house will publicise the finalised plans by distribution to a wider circle of Party committees, as well as to the book trade and libraries.

Republic and regional (*oblast'*) Party secretariats include in their establishments a 'secretary for ideological matters', whose sphere of responsibility includes publishing, as well as science, education and cultural activities.[29] Relationships between a provincial publishing-house and its local Party authorities have been illustrated by the director of the Tsentral'no-Chernozemnoe house, which acts as local publisher to five *oblasti*. He instances, as approaches made in the course of 'a normal working day', the Belgorod Party *obkom* (regional committee) proposing publication of a book, *Geroi-belgorodtsy* (*Heroes of Belgorod*), as a reissue, since 30 000 copies have quickly sold out; a secretary from the Tambov *obkom* suggesting a book on Party organisational work and promising a manuscript shortly; and the Lipetsk *obkom* thanking the house for the issue of two recent works and asking if it can publicise the work of animal husbandry complexes and a local gallery.[30] The same publishing-house, when it was formed in 1964, had sought the advice of all five Party *obkomy* in selecting a staff from among the best workers in the several houses it replaced. Like others, this house took Party advice on subjects to be dealt with, and on authors to be approached, in preparing its annual publication plan; but local Party organs are not infrequently criticised for obliging a publishing-house to issue ill-judged works of the organs' own choice outside the scope of its publishing plan.[31]

The publishing-house's own Party organisation, and the Party secretary in particular, is expected to participate fully in the house's management, including staff selection, and to exercise supervision of its activities in the Party's name. All Party members – who will, of course, normally include the director and his senior staff – are required to ensure the Party's 'leading role' in the work of the enterprise, but the 'right of supervision' (*pravo kontrolya*) tends in practice in most enterprises to be exercised by the Party secretary. He is not subordinated to the director, but to the local Party committee, and may demand information or documents from the director in order to fulfil his function. The Party bureau can also require reports from the house's departments on progress in plan fulfilment, in order to discuss improvements with them.[32] Proposals for important organisational changes, such as the adoption of a system of 'internal *khozraschet*', are expected to be discussed at meetings of the Party membership before being put to the personnel as a whole.[33] All Party members, on the other hand, are subject to Party discipline as well as to the normal sanctions against employees: the director of the trade-union publishing-house Profizdat, for example, was severely censured by the Party Control Committee in 1975 for alleged drunkenness on a visit abroad, an indulgent attitude to breaches of discipline among his staff, and for accepting a fee from a foreign publisher. He was subsequently dismissed from his post by the house's superior organ.[34]

3.3. *The Party in printing and the book trade*

Party decisions and supervision affect the printing industry and the book trade through similar channels at all levels. The Central Committee's Department of Propaganda and its Department of Engineering both have a degree of responsibility for the development of the printing industry. Initiatives for the construction of new printing plant often emanate from, or are approved by, Party organs in consultation with local soviets and the State Committee for Publishing.[35] Party regulation of the book trade can be equally far-reaching: it was the Central Committee of the Communist Party of Moldavia which decreed that all the bookselling outlets of consumer cooperatives in the republic should be transferred to a single system administered by the republic's State Committee for Publishing.[36]

Printing and bookselling enterprises likewise each have their own Party element: the Leningrad book trade organisation reported 200 Party members and candidate members among its staff in 1971, including thirty-two bookshop managers. A particular Party concern is that political literature should be made as readily available as possible. Book trade staff are advised to finalise orders to publishers for such material only after consultation with Party organisations. Party committees' propaganda departments review and, where necessary, alter book orders placed by the Party educational institutions.[37]

3.4. *The Party as publisher*

The Party's own publishing requirements, as an organisation, are extensive and demanding. It had (in 1971) direct control of the central publishing-houses Pravda and Politizdat, and of seventy-eight local houses.[38] The bulk of these houses' output consists of newspapers, journals, and instructional literature for the Party educational system, but Politizdat is also a book publisher on a large scale, with the exclusive right (from 1976) to issue all textbooks for higher and secondary special education in the subjects of Party history, Marxist–Leninist philosophy, political economy and scientific communism.[39] One-third of the Party's direct income is claimed by its officials to come from deductions from the profits of its publishing-houses, with the balance coming from membership dues.[40] However, as McNeal has shown, the proportions claimed are probably misleading, since the Party apparently derives a good deal of additional income from the state.[41]

All publishers handling Party material are required to observe the highest possible standards of accuracy and promptitude. Any manuscript dealing with the work of a Party organ must be checked with that body before being accepted for publication;[42] any matter quoted from Party and government statements (and from the Marxist–Leninist classics) must be verified by the author from the original; and all pronouncements by Party and state leaders (and Marxist–Leninist classics again) must not only be read in page proof, but proofread afresh at every 50 000 copies printed. At the same time, the table of norms for publishing-house editors handling official statements and Marxist–Leninist classics envisages faster processing for them than for any other type of socio-political literature (a rate of seventeen publisher's sheets per month, compared with four sheets for mass political literature), presumably because editorial revision will not extend to the content of the text.[43] Politizdat objected to proposals made in 1972 (and since partly adopted) to bring forward the pre-publication period allowed for collecting book trade orders, because this would make it more difficult for them to react quickly to Party and government decisions in the works which they published. Another example of the priority given to Party publications is that, while book deliveries to libraries by their supply agencies are normally made once or twice a month, Party documents and leaders' statements, as well as topical political literature, must be transmitted to libraries as soon as received.[44]

3.5. *The Party's exercise of its authority*

In their supervision of publishing, as of other industries, Party organs are not expected to concern themselves with the minutiae of day-to-day administration, although many are said in fact to do so. Within a publishing-house, the primary Party organisation and its superior Party organs appear to give closest attention to the house's general policy over the character of its publications, to the selection of important or controversial manuscripts, to senior staff appointments, and to overall efficiency and economic performance. The union or republic State Committee for Publishing, as the government ministry directly in charge of the publishing industry, shares some authority with the Party in these matters, while detailed planning and budgeting, production scheduling and relations with printers and the book trade are guided much more exclusively by regulations from the State Committee. Party intervention in these areas is most likely to be in order to settle disputes, to clear bottlenecks in supplies or production, or to carry through a campaign or programme requiring special measures.

Comprehensive as the Party's resources are for controlling the activity and products of Soviet publishing, communication between the Party and the publishing industry cannot consist merely of directives issued by the former to the latter. Some at least of the initiatives on organisational and economic matters described above can only have been taken by the Party organs as a direct result of representations made by publishing-houses or by the state publishing administration, with the support of the lower-level Party organisations. Consultation between publishers and their local Party committees is usually on a fairly informal, day-to-day basis; and the central publishing-houses, and the State Committee for Publishing itself, must have sufficient access to the Central Committee, through the Department of Propaganda, for proposals and pressures on at least some issues to be directed there. It seems likely, furthermore, that the Department of Propaganda will on occasion be prepared to support the claims of the publishing industry against those of other industries or other sections of the Secretariat. Exercising its supra-departmental authority in this manner, the Party apparatus carries out its tasks of resolving disputes over political and economic priorities, regulating competition for limited resources, and at the same time maintaining its standing as the principal initiator of change, in publishing as in other spheres of Soviet life.

4

The government apparatus

Although Soviet publishing activity at every stage is subject to Party initiatives, supervision and intervention, the publishing industry, considered as an economic and administrative entity, ranks alongside other branches of industry in being subordinated to a central government department of ministry standing which exercises continuous planning authority and close control over its work. The State Committee for Publishing, Printing and the Book Trade carries on this function subject to existing legislation and to the scrutiny of the Supreme Soviet, the Council of Ministers of the USSR and the Central Committee of the Party, and with the participation of several other government agencies. This chapter examines the roles of the State Committee for Publishing and other government bodies at all-union and republic level in regulating the industry's operations and products. The place of each of the entities concerned in these activities is first characterised separately, and this is followed by an account of their parts as played over time in determining the nature and flow of the nation's book production.

4.1. *The highest organs of government*

The Supreme Soviet, the USSR's highest formal legislative body, exercises its powers of scrutiny over the publishing industry partly through the commissions for education, science and culture of its two chambers, which hold joint sessions to review achievements and shortcomings and hear a report from the chairman of the State Committee for Publishing;[1] and partly by the consideration of annual and longer-term economic plans, including those for publishing, by a full session of the Supreme Soviet. The Presidium of the Supreme Soviet appoints the chairmen of the State Committees of the Council of Ministers of the USSR, including that of the State Committee for Publishing.

The USSR Council of Ministers, of which the chairman of the State Committee for Publishing is ex-officio a member, is responsible for approving the appointment of deputy chairmen and members of the board (*kollegiya*) of this committee, and of other committees of the same rank. It also lays down the basic statutes (*polozheniya*) of ministries and state committees, which specify their rights and duties, and it approves the outline administrative structure of each and the organisation of their central staff establishments. Its other powers, as they apply to publishing, reserve to it the final approval of some of the most important operating regulations under which the State Committee and publishers work, and of the industry's annual economic plan. These regulations and plans are normally placed before the Council of Ministers after preparation and drafting by the State Committee for Publishing, but may be modified. The requirement that approval by the Council of Ministers must be secured, and secured frequently after some delay or alteration, combined with other deadlines to be met later in the measure's timetable, is by no means a negligible factor in policy implementation, in particular as it affects the efforts of the State Committee and publishers to adhere to their production plans.

The councils of ministers of the Soviet republics have comparable powers to approve the plans of publishers administered by their own republics' state committees for publishing. They also confirm the scales of fees to be paid to authors in each republic, a matter which is considered to arise from the civil legislation of the republics rather than of the union. The Council of Ministers of the RSFSR has to agree the scales for authors writing for the central publishing-houses, with the approval of the CPSU Central Committee, as described in the previous chapter. The state committees for publishing of the republics are empowered to make instructions for the detailed application of the fee scales. The councils of ministers of the republics exercise certain powers over their local publishers which fall to the USSR State Committee for Publishing in the case of central publishing-houses, notably the discretion to increase book retail prices in individual cases (by up to 20 per cent) to avoid losses, and to make certain variations in the composition of publishing-houses' incentive funds.

4.2. *The State Committee for Publishing*

The State Committee of the Council of Ministers of the USSR for Publishing, Printing and the Book Trade (Goskomizdat SSSR) is the most recent product of decades of effort by Party and government to achieve comprehensive control of publishing activity in the Soviet Union.[2] Its direct descent can be traced back to the creation in 1949 of a Chief Administration for Printing and Publishing (Glavpoligrafizdat) attached to the USSR Council of Ministers, replacing the looser Association of State Publishing-Houses (OGIZ) which had existed since 1930. Glavpoligrafizdat was subordinated to the USSR Ministry of Culture in 1953, and until 1963 the administration of publishing, printing and the book trade remained the responsibility of a variety of departments within that ministry. In 1963 the sector was placed in the charge of a new State Committee for the Press of the USSR Council of Ministers, which two years later changed its title and became the Committee for the Press attached to the USSR Council of Ministers, and assumed its present designation on 1 August 1972.

Most Soviet state committees (as distinct from ministries) have a planning, organisational or coordinating role in relation to other government departments, as is the case with the State Planning Committee (Gosplan), the State Committee for Labour and Wages, and the State Committee for Science and Technology. Others, including the State Committee for Publishing, combine the direct administration of one branch of industry or culture with a measure of coordinating authority over enterprises or institutions subordinated to other ministries or departments. The change in the State Committee's title in 1972, and in particular the fact that it is now again a committee 'of', instead of 'attached to', the Council of Ministers, indicates a slight rise in formal status,[3] and has been accompanied by an extension of powers for an administrative apparatus which, in organisation and leading personnel, has been little altered. These additional powers allow the State Committee more comprehensive coordination of publishing plans, on an all-union scale and regardless of the departmental subordination of the publishers; closer control of all new construction and development programmes in the printing industry; and the authority to allocate all printing capacity.[4]

The State Committee's statute gives it responsibility for the direction (*rukovodstvo*) of publishing, printing and the book trade throughout the Soviet Union, and the general supervision (*kontrol'*) of the content of all types of publication.[5] As a union–republican administration, it controls directly many of the central publishing-houses, major printing enterprises, and the central wholesale organisation of its own book trade network, while delegating to state committees for publishing in each republic, and to publishing administrations at regional (*krai* and *oblast'*) level, control of local publishers and bookselling organisations, and of the smaller printing enterprises. In 1974, 154 of the 198 Soviet book publishing-houses were under the direct control of the union-level State Committee or its local subordinate committees. Between them they were producing about 70 per cent of book copies published, though only some 30 per cent of titles.[6] (Much of the balance in the number of titles is accounted for by publications in small editions produced by organisations which are not publishing-houses proper.) The State Committee coordinates the annual and longer-term plans of all organisations with the right to issue printed matter (except scientific and technical information services), and drafts the overall economic plans for the sector for incorporation into the national planning procedures, except for the newspaper and journal output of the Party's own organs. It may modify a publisher's area of specialisation (which it does in practice in consultation with the Party), and may express an opinion on the foundation or winding-up of a publishing-house – on which the Party authorities will again take the final decision.

In matters of supply, the State Committee undertakes the distribution within the sector of the paper allocated to it (the global amount of paper so allocated being determined by the State Planning Committee), and divides available printing capacity between publishers to enable them to complete their approved production plans. It prepares for approval by the republics' councils of ministers all scales of authors' fees, and confirms all types of standard contract between authors and publishers. Retail and wholesale prices for all kinds of printed matter, new and second-hand, are fixed by it in consultation with the State Committee for Prices, as well as prices for printing inks and type (though not paper), and for all printing work. It sets the salary scales of publishing and other staff in the sector, in agreement with the State Committee for Labour and Wages, lays down the standards which determine the size of each publisher's staff establishment, and is in charge of the professional training of personnel in all three subsectors.

The State Committee for Publishing has two consultative organs attached to it, the Publishing Council and the Technical Council. The former's membership includes senior scholars, publishing-house staff, and representatives from a number of ministries. It is chaired by the chairman of the State Committee for Publishing, and staff from the CPSU Central Committee Secretariat attend its sessions, which discuss major issues of publishing policy. The meeting of 11 March 1975, which was reported in exceptional detail, dealt with three topics: the determination of optimal proportions between the output of different kinds of literature; the publication of scientific and technical literature in the light of the 24th Party Congress decisions on scientific progress; and the application of automated management systems to book publishing.[7] The Technical Council examines and approves the basic lines of technical policy in the printing industry, and overall plans for research, development and construction.

The State Committee for Publishing is headed by a chairman appointed by the Presidium of the Supreme Soviet, with (in 1976) a first deputy chairman and at least four deputy chairmen, and a board appointed by the USSR Council of Ministers.[8] The chairman, who is also chairman of the State Committee's board, carries personal responsibility for the Committee's fulfilment of its duties, and determines the areas of responsibility to be borne by his principal subordinates. Since the 25th Party Congress, the chairman has been a full member of the CPSU Central Committee. Although the board is expected to discuss all important matters affecting the sector, it is strictly speaking an advisory body, whose recommendations can be put into effect only through an order issued by the chairman. Within the limits of existing legislation and of the Council of Ministers' decrees, the chairman has discretion to make orders and instructions without the board's advice, or even against that advice, but in the latter case the Council of Ministers must be informed. The State Committee's highest reaches of decision-making thus follow the principle of one-man management (*edinonachalie*) observed by most Soviet ministries, rather than the collective responsibility (*kollegial'nost'*) exercised by the Council of Ministers itself and by a number of other state committees, such as Gosplan.

There is a strong tendency for the highest officials of the State Committee for Publishing to be drawn from among those who have made careers in Party and ideological work, rather than in publishing narrowly defined. The present (1977) chairman, B. I. Stukalin, who was chairman of the Committee for the Press before its change of title, came to that post as a former deputy chief editor of *Pravda* and, earlier, section head in the Department of Propaganda of the Central Committee.[9] The latest deputy chairman to be appointed, A. A. Nebenzya, has had a career of thirty years in Komsomol and Party work, rising to be a secretary in the Volgograd *obkom*.[10] The bulk of the State Committee's board members, however, consist of the heads of its main departments, its three chief editors, and representatives from other ministries and organisations.

Matters coming before the board include, besides questions involving the industry as a whole, its subsectors and enterprises, many discussions on single works, series, and literature on specific subjects. All new publishers' series, indeed, may be launched only with the State Committee's agreement, and the same condition applies to multi-volume publications considered of less importance than those whose preparation requires the authorisation of the CPSU Central Committee. (A recent example is the thirty-volume edition of Chekhov's works, published by Nauka.) The board reviews the quality and coverage of recent publishing in particular subjects, such as atheism or socialist competition, and confirms recommendations prepared by the State Committee's staff on the selection and editing of types of literature felt to require improvement in these respects. For example, its recommendations on the publication of memoirs in 1975 gave criteria for more judicious selection, and stipulated that manuscripts of memoirs must be considered by the publishing-house's editorial council and the appropriate creative union before being approved.[11] The board's approval is required for the annual and longer-term plans for publications in each subject, as well as for lists of titles planned on particularly topical themes: immediately after the April 1973 plenum of the Central Committee, for instance, the board sanctioned a list of 'especially significant' works on the USSR's foreign policy to be published during the coming year.

The departmental structure of the State Committee for Publishing is shown in table 1. The chief editorial offices (*glavnye redaktsii*) exercise the State Committee's supervision over the central publishing-houses subordinated directly to it. The Chief Editorial Office for Scientific and Technical Literature, for example, has charge of the seventeen central publishers specialising in the subject areas concerned. Each of the chief editorial offices is allotted an output plan based on the production targets of its publishing-houses, and the greater part of its work consists of checking the suitability of these enterprises' proposed publication plans from the viewpoints of subject coverage, duplication and economic feasibility, and of

Table 1. *Departmental structure of the State Committee for Publishing*

1. Chief Editorial Office for Socio-Political Literature*
2. Chief Editorial Office for Fiction*
3. Chief Editorial Office for Scientific and Technical Literature*
4. Chief Administration for Combined Thematic Planning and Coordination
5. Chief Administration for Republic and Oblast' Publishers
6. Chief Administration for the Printing Industry (Glavpoligrafiya)
7. Chief Administration for the Book Trade and Book Propaganda (Glavkniga)*
8. Economic Planning and Financial Administration (ranking as a chief administration)
9. Technical Administration (ranking as a chief administration)
10. Chief Administration for Design and Capital Construction
11. Chief Administration for Material and Technical Supply (Glavsnabsbyt)*
12. State Inspectorate for the Quality of Publications
13. Administration for Personnel
14. Administration for Accounting and Auditing
15. Administration for Labour Organisation and Wages
16. Administration for International Relations
17. General Administration (*upravlenie delami*)
18. Department of the Chief Artist
19. First Department (*Pervyi otdel*. Believed to be staff of the Committee for State Security or KGB. See note 13.)
20. Main Information and Computing Centre
21. Chief Administration for the Publication and Export Delivery of Soviet Literature for the Foreign Reader (set up in 1977, see 8.6)
22. Publishing Council and Technical Council
23. All-Union Industrial Association of Printing Enterprises of Union Subordination (Soyuzpoligrafprom)*
24. All-Union State Industrial Association 'Soyuzuchetizdat'*
25. The newspaper *Knizhnoe obozrenie*
26. The journals *V mire knig, Poligrafiya, Detskaya literatura*

* On *khozraschet*

Sources
Trud i zarabotnaya plata rabotnikov izdatel'stv i redaktsii zhurnalov (M., 1973), pp. 56–7.
V. A. Markus, *Organizatsiya i ekonomika izdatel'skogo dela*, 3rd ed. (M., 1976). pp. 26–7.

monitoring the fulfilment of plans subsequently approved.[12] The 20 per cent reserve of paper and printing capacity in publishers' annual plans must be laid out on publications which have been approved by the chief editorial office.

In addition, the chief editorial offices are expected to maintain a general overview and assessment of all Soviet publishing in their respective subject fields, and to lead the longer-term planning of material issued in these subjects, in consultation with the Chief Administration for Republic and Oblast' Publishers. At least one chief editorial office, that for scientific and technical literature, has established a council of the directors of all publishers subordinated directly to it, who join staff from the State Committee and representatives from the printing industry and book trade to study matters of general concern, most importantly new trends in their subjects which should be catered for by publication. The same office has added a new technique to its reviewing procedures by obtaining an analysis by experts of recent publications on a special topic issued by several publishers, enabling an assessment of the quality of coverage and recommendations for further books to be made.[14]

The Economic Planning and Financial Administration is the point within the State Committee's structure at which economic and financial data for the performance of the publishing, printing and bookselling subsectors are brought together. It prepares the draft economic plans for the sector as a whole for submission, through the State Committee's board, to the Council of Ministers and Gosplan; and it has an important (though not the only) voice in the allocation to publishers of subsidies from the state budget, the setting of bank credit ceilings, and the redistribution and use of profits and financial reserves.[15]

The Chief Administration for Combined Thematic Planning and Coordination was created in 1972 to undertake the State Committee's broadened responsibility for coordination of titles and publishing plans (described in detail in 4.5). It has also since 1975 compiled 'overall plans' of titles for the USSR as a whole for submission to the State Committee's board, and plans for books in subjects regarded by the Party and the government as being of particular importance. Both types of plan are based exclusively on publishers' own proposed plans for publication and editorial preparation, and the work done on them by both the chief administration and the board appears to be intended primarily to eradicate duplication and save paper, rather than to instigate significant changes in the nature of the coverage as represented by the sum of publishers' proposals.[16]

The Chief Administration for Material and Technical Supply (Glavsnabsbyt) prepares the annual supply plan for the sector from the figures confirmed with Gosplan and with the Council of Ministers for publishing output (in millions of sheet-copies), total and specialised printing capacity, and provision of paper, binding materials, printing ink and type metal. After approval by the board, Glavsnabsbyt submits the appropriate claims to Gosplan and the other agencies producing or distributing the supplies in question. It then allocates the material within the sector, in consultation with other departments of the State Committee for Publishing, dealing directly with the consuming enterprises – publishers and printers – under contracts between itself and them.[17]

4.3. *Republic and local publishing administration*

The state committees for publishing of the union republics, and the publishing administrations at autonomous republic, *krai* and *oblast'* level, follow the 'dual subordination' principle of many Soviet ministries in being subordinated both to their own republic's council of ministers (or *oblast'* or *krai* executive committee) and to the union-level State Committee for Publishing. It is the latter which, as has been shown, determines many of the general policies and operating conditions for publishing throughout the USSR; and it may, within this hierarchy of subordination, give instructions to the republic and local publishing administrations on many matters both general and detailed – and, through them, to any publisher under their jurisdiction. In 1973, for example, reviewing progress in raising the profitability of publishing, it instructed all the republics' state committees for publishing to investigate the operations of all publishing-houses making planned losses, and to identify ways of reducing subsidies.[18] Again, after considering the publishing plan of the Kazakhstan house for 1976, the USSR State Committee for Publishing, while approving it in general, instructed the publishers to place greater emphasis on works which dealt with the Party's foreign policy and which laid bare bourgeois philosophical and economic theories.[19]

In the opposite direction, the republic state committees for publishing will need to seek approval from the USSR State Committee for important measures which they wish to undertake. A senior official of the State Committee for Publishing of the Kazakh SSR complained in 1975 that his committee had several times proposed the establishment of a publishing-house for children's literature in the republic (a step which would require the approval of the Party as well as that of the USSR State Committee), but so far had been given no decision.[20]

The statutes and structure of the republic and local publishing administrations reflect their much more limited sphere of action. For the publishing-houses administered by them, and the other bodies within their area granted the right to publish, they approve and coordinate publication plans and the associated arrangements for paper, other supplies and printing; but this does not remove the obligation that the subject-matter of all books and pamphlets should be 'coordinated' again by the USSR State Committee for Publishing against its information about publication plans throughout the Soviet Union. There is some indication that, in republics with only a few publishing-houses, the state committees for publishing concern themselves more closely with individual works, to the extent that their staff read the more important manuscripts under consideration by publishers and express opinions on their suitability, before the publisher accepts them for publication.[21] In the case of works proposed for publication by organisations other than publishing-houses, the state committees for publishing are explicitly granted the right to demand manuscripts and referees' reports before approving publication plans.[22]

4.4. *Other participating organs*

Among the central ministries and state committees, that with the most extensive influence on the activities of the State Committee for Publishing is the State Planning Committee (Gosplan). As the central economic planning agency, Gosplan allocates, on an all-union scale, the raw materials and products judged by the government to be of greatest importance in the economy. Of especial importance to the publishing industry is the fact that these include paper.

The State Planning Committee is of course subject to the authority of the USSR Council of Ministers and the CPSU Central Committee, and may be instructed by either or both to alter its allocations in support of a higher policy decision. When the Central

Committee expressed concern in 1970 over the amount of printed matter produced by ministries and other bodies which were not publishing-houses, the State Planning Committee was ordered to restrict the amount of paper allocated to those bodies, and to transfer the stocks thus freed to the Committee for the Press (as it then was) to increase the output of textbooks.[23] Materials not allocated by the State Planning Committee are supplied to the publishing industry by the State Committee for Material–Technical Supply (Gossnab SSSR) and other ministries and departments. The annual production plan for publishing throughout the USSR has to be submitted to the State Planning Committee by the State Committee for Publishing, for confirmation of the proposed planning indicators. The principles for the transfer of enterprises in the publishing industry to the new planning and incentive system in the early 1970s also had to be approved in detail by the State Planning Committee, and the transfer subsequently of each publishing-house has required the same sanction.

Other central government organs which have a voice in publishing policy include the Ministry of Finance of the USSR, which, with the ministries of finance of the republics, inspects publishing-houses' financial plans – often altering publishers' estimates considerably in the process.[24] The Ministry of Finance also takes part in decisions affecting the finances of publishing as a whole, such as the revision of book retail prices which was called for by the Central Committee in 1970. The State Committee for Prices, which likewise took part in this latter revision, maintains checks on publishers' price setting. (On one occasion, the Kolos publishing-house was found to have illegally raised prices on five books by an additional face value of 39 000r.)[25] Agreement from the State Committee for Labour and Wages is required for many regulations affecting salaries, bonuses and staffing standards; and special conditions applying to contracts between publishers and booksellers have needed the confirmation of the State Arbitration.

Particularly in matters affecting employment, salaries and incentives, publishing administrators are obliged to act in consultation or agreement with trade-union organisations, from all-union down to enterprise level. For example, where a publishing-house fails to meet its annual publication plan in some important respect, its superior organ may reduce the amount of profits transferred to the house's incentive fund, but only with the agreement of the Central Committee of the Union of Cultural Workers, or its republic equivalent.[26] Further examples of trade-union participation are given in chapter 5.

Organs of ministry rank whose powers affect only certain kinds of publication are the union and republic ministries of general education, the USSR Ministry of Higher and Secondary Special Education, and the State Committee for Science and Technology. The education ministries' rigorous control of the planning and content of textbooks and other educational material will be dealt with in detail in 9.4. The State Committee for Science and Technology has special responsibility for scientific and technical information services, and has the same authority in confirming (subject to Central Committee approval) the right of information services to publish, and the plans under which they do so, as that which the State Committee for Publishing exercises over other bodies allowed to issue publications.

Another government organ of comparable status – the censorship – affects publishing activity most directly at the level of the individual publishing-house, and is considered in 5.9.

4.5. *The coordination process*

The process of coordination is applied by the State Committee for Publishing to works proposed for publication. It is primarily a first check by central authority on each book title that reaches the point of being considered by a publisher. The coordination process is distinct from the annual and longer-term planning of books to be issued which is undertaken by the State Committee and the publishers. Those parts of the publishing plans which identify individual titles either consist of works already coordinated and approved, or remain tentative to the extent that they include any projects or uncompleted manuscripts which have not yet undergone coordination. The coordination work of the State Committee for Publishing is a preliminary to the inclusion of a manuscript or author's proposal in a publisher's plan for editorial preparation and subsequently publication. Since 1974 it has been applied to all publications, regardless of the body issuing them. (Regulations until that date excluded Party, government, trade-union and Komsomol publications.)[27] The State Committee's coordination work is also quite distinct from the censorship applied by Glavlit to a work immediately before it is printed, as described in 5.9.

Immediately after a publishing-house has decided that it wishes to issue a work which has been submitted to it in manuscript or proposed to it by an author, and before a contract with the author is signed, a special form giving details of the work is forwarded to the State Committee for Publishing (through the local publishing administration, if the publisher is under their jurisdiction). The Chief Administration for Combined Thematic Planning and Coordination, in consultation with the appropriate chief editorial office, may then instruct approval or refusal of the work; postponement of publication; a reduction (the regulations do not provide for an increase) in the proposed edition size; 'etcetera', which probably covers transfer to another publisher or modifications to the work's theme or approach.[28] The Chief Administration received coordination forms for 45 554 titles for publishers' 1977 plans. Of these, 5109 were ordered to be postponed, over 1000 to be rejected, and over 300 to be reduced in length.[29] The stated guidelines for these instructions are the maintenance of defined areas of specialisation by publishing-houses; the avoidance of duplication in subject-matter; and economy in the consumption of paper. Computer-produced bulletins listing respectively proposals received and titles 'coordinated' (and therefore likely to be published) are circulated for information to publishers and other interested organisations. The publishing-house may not conclude a contract with the author until the work has been listed in the bulletin of titles coordinated. This procedure is now a component of the ASU–PECHAT' automated management system described in greater detail in 4.7. A second coordination check on the same principles is carried out when the State Committee examines publishers' plans for editorial preparation each year: it was claimed that as many as 1500 titles were excluded from draft plans at this stage in 1974.[30]

The State Committee for Publishing asserted in 1976 that some publishing-houses and local publishing administrations were adopting a mistaken attitude to the central coordination process, resenting what they regarded as outside interference in their plans and attempting to assert their 'independence'.[31] The demand by a deputy chairman of the State Committee in the same year that some publishers must cease their practice of altering approved publication plans by 20 or 30 per cent suggests that the coordination process is still not fully enforceable.[32]

4.6. *The planning cycle*

It is the administrative work devoted to planning and controlling the flow of printed matter towards the reading public, in sequences of events which are repeated either for each title or for each year, which forms by far the greater part of the total work of the State Committee for Publishing, and of the State Planning Committee's participation in the publishing operation. Other duties, such as the preparation of new regulations, and intervention or consultation in special cases, appear to consume much less effort than do the preparation, supervision and review of publishers' output from year to year.

The longer-term planning work of the State Committee for Publishing (that is, for periods of more than one year) includes a series of overall plans by subject for titles or topics intended to be treated over the duration of a five-year plan: for example, the 'Combined publication plan for scientific and technical literature' and 'Classical and contemporary literature of the peoples of the USSR'. Like the 'overall plans' prepared annually, these depend heavily for their content on publishers' own plans and proposals. Cases have been made for even longer-term plans of this kind, extending over ten or even fifteen years, but the idea has been strongly contested by scientific publishers and those houses such as Politizdat which prefer a five-year maximum period to coincide with Party congresses, the decisions of which will have a marked effect on the content of their publications. The State Committee for Publishing is, however, supporting forecasting studies of output and demand up to 1990 and beyond, some results of which are examined in 9.10.

The State Committee's most concrete and detailed long-term plan, subject to the greatest number of constraints, is that prepared in collaboration with the State Planning Committee for incorporation into each national five-year economic plan. The State Planning Committee's approach to the five-year plan takes little account of the subject-matter of the publications to be issued, and none at all of separate titles. It begins with, on the one hand, the anticipated total available printing capacity (including specialised facilities and capacity at the USSR's disposal in other socialist countries under agreement), and expected supplies of paper and other materials.[33] In placing against these physical limits the figures prepared by the State Committee for Publishing showing the potential demand for each type of publication, the State Planning Committee will normally be able to satisfy the latter only partially, although priorities established by the State Committee for Publishing will determine the degree to which demand for each category is met. The amount and varieties of printing paper available are likely to remain for the foreseeable future the ultimate determinant of the total number of publications which can be issued, as suggested in 7.3.

For the ninth Five-Year Plan (1971–5), for the first time, the State Committee for Publishing prepared five-year plans for every publishing, printing and bookselling enterprise under its jurisdiction, within the overall limitations agreed with Gosplan, broken down into annual plans (although these latter are subject to amendment and re-confirmation before the beginning of each plan year, after which they become legally binding). This was a preliminary to alterations in the annual planning process, also undertaken in consultation with Gosplan. Since 1973, within the constraints of paper supply and printing capacity, the sector has begun to change to the use of publishers' approved annual publication plans (*tematicheskie plany*) as a basis for the annual planning of all three subsectors. These publication plans, or rather the production and sale of titles included in them, are now criteria for judging the fulfilment of publishers' and printers' financial plans and book trade organisations' turnover plans. This contrasts with previous practice under which printers' and booksellers' plans had no link with the titles which publishers wished to publish, and hence gave no incentive for printing and selling the greatest possible number of titles in the publishing plan, but on the contrary encouraged both printer and bookseller to give priority to those books which were most economically advantageous to the fulfilment of their own plans for output and financial performance.[34]

The timing of the various phases in the planning sequence was also changed, in 1976, to enable financial plans and production schedules to be finalised by the publisher after the year's publication plan had been confirmed, rather than before, as was previously the usual case. Under the revised arrangements for central publishing-houses,[35] the drafting of their proposed publication plans (from previously coordinated and approved manuscripts and authors' proposals), and the approval of these by the State Committee for Publishing, is expected to be completed during the second half of the year *before* the year immediately preceding the plan year, to enable copies of the publication plan (with a descriptive paragraph on each title) to be circulated to the book trade by 1 January in the year preceding the plan year. The wholesale bookselling organisations will then be allowed seventy-five days in which to collect pre-publication orders through their retail networks, sending their estimates of the number of copies of each title required back to each publisher by 15 March. Within the next month, publishers must compare the amounts ordered with the combination of paper supplies, printing facilities, and figures for title and copy output and for economic performance which the State Committee for Publishing has laid down for them under the five-year plan. They make amendments to edition sizes accordingly (usually by reducing them, since demand for most types of literature exceeds what publishers can expect to supply), and send these amendments for confirmation to the appropriate chief editorial office in the State Committee for Publishing by 15 April. By 1 May, the confirmed plans are communicated to the bookselling organisations, and by the same date publishers inform the printers allocated to them of the confirmed plan, and of their printing requirements arising from it. After consultation with the printers, the publishers are expected to give their chief editorial office at the State Committee for Publishing a statement of their anticipated output in quantitative terms, and of any alterations in staff requirements, by 10 May, and to place detailed claims for printing facilities, paper and other materials by 25 May.

The chief editorial offices, the Chief Administration for the Printing Industry, and the Economic Planning and Financial Administration then combine to prepare draft overall economic and production plans for the entire sector, which are examined by the board of the State Committee for Publishing and submitted to the Council of Ministers and Gosplan by 15 June. When the economic plan has been approved by the Council of Ministers, and when Gosplan has confirmed the indicator figures for production, the State Committee for Publishing transmits the revised and approved plans to each publisher, printer and bookselling organisation, who alter their detailed production schedules and financial plans accordingly. The State Committee compiles and confirms overall publishing plans by subject before 15 October. Any necessary changes in the allocation of printing facilities and paper supplies (which must have the State Committee's approval) can be inserted into publishers' and printers' plans up to 20 December, in order to provide for late alterations to the publishing plans or revised figures for journal subscriptions. Finally, all annual contracts between publisher and printer, and between publisher and bookselling organs, must be concluded by 25 December of the year before the plan year. Quarterly and monthly production plans agreed between publisher and printer must be notified to the State Committee for Publishing regularly during the course of the plan year.

This revised timetable was introduced experimentally into the planning of the two central houses Ekonomika and Mysl', and several republic houses, from 1974. A review of the results, after planning for 1974 and 1975 was completed, indicated that publishing plans were much more likely to be met in full under the new arrangements, but that, as under the previous timetable, any slippage at the beginning of the sequence (such as delay in approving the draft publication plan before its circulation to the book trade) jeopardised the accuracy of the orders collected by the booksellers and threatened the timing of all later stages in the process. Even by early 1976, however, the new timetable had not been extended to most publishing-houses; and many publishing plans were being distributed to the book trade as late as August of the year preceding the plan year, with the result that edition sizes could not be finalised until November of that year, although claims for printing capacity had had to be placed in the previous July.[36]

The state committees for publishing in the union republics handle the annual planning process for publishers subordinated to them in a similar manner, but with the additional stages of submitting their publishers' approved manuscripts and authors' proposals for co-ordination by the USSR State Committee for Publishing, and subsequently obtaining the latter's approval for their publishers' and their own overall plans by subject. In the Ukrainian SSR, the formal force of law has been given to the requirement that the annual publishing plan be used as a basis by booksellers and printers as well as by publishers, and any title expected to lose more than 5000r. must be specially authorised by the republic's State Committee for Publishing.[37]

4.7. *Automated systems in publishing administration*

The high degree of central control maintained over the Soviet publishing industry has compelled the State Committee for Publishing to assume many of the policy-making, budgeting and production control functions which would be performed at the level of the individual publishing-house in the West. Further, the State Committee has had to erect additional administrative structures in order to permit coherent planning and coordination of the entire publishing–printing–bookselling sector. In particular, priorities must be established for the distribution of limited paper stocks, and this distribution must be matched up with the publication plans of over 200 publishers, and with the printing capacity and equipment of over 3000 printing enterprises.

There are obvious attractions in employing computer-based systems for routines of this kind, which require extensive sets of calculations and listings, repeated at regular intervals. This type of task appears to have been regarded as the most urgent operational requirement when the State Committee for Publishing began the development of an 'automated management system' for book publishing in 1972. However, the scope and scale of the system as now planned (in 1977) extend far beyond these immediate objectives, and have no parallel in Western publishing. Besides making the calculations on which are based the production and economic plans for the entire sector, the system is to monitor the fulfilment of these plans and provide regular information on the economic position of each publishing-house and of the publishing industry as a whole. Furthermore, it is to accept data on every book title published or in preparation, and on every proposal submitted to a publisher, to help in avoiding duplication of coverage, record authors' specialities and reveal topics in need of published treatment. Data input from book trade organisations is also to be accepted, to improve stock control and produce analyses of demand and sales. By early 1976, 48.8 million roubles was stated to have been allocated for the introduction of computer-based management systems into the sector, although this figure also included the provision of smaller systems, such as those governing technical processes in a single printing combine, or supplying internal management information in a single publishing-house.[38]

It is believed that four subsystems of the central ASU–PECHAT′ system began operation in 1975, using computer centres established at the State Committee for Publishing and at the All-Union Book Chamber: those covering accounting, personnel and financial records, and the first stage of that handling the coordination of manuscripts. The automation of the coordinating process is the first phase in the introduction of the subsystem ASU–PECHAT′–IZDAT, which will cater for the publishing subsector.[39] At a later stage in this subsystem's development, all authors' proposals to publishers for works to be written (some 40 000 annually) will also be communicated to a computer-held file at the State Committee's information centre. This will allow checking for duplication of treatment at an early stage, and will at the same time build up a file of subjects proposed for treatment in print and of authors prepared to tackle them. It is further intended that data on the subject-matter of manuscripts whose preparation has been approved should be supplied to the State Committee in considerably more detail than at present, possibly employing the same classification as that used in ASU–PECHAT′–BIBLIOGRAF, described below. It is hoped that these bodies of information will furnish the basis for forecasting the proportions occupied by different types of publication in the total output of printed matter; enable gaps in coverage to be identified; and help to reveal topics whose increasing or lessening importance ought to be reflected in the amount and variety of literature issued.

The printing industry is to be provided with a subsystem entitled ASU–PECHAT′–PROM, which is intended to store data on paper stocks and other supplies, and on available printing capacity. It is anticipated that this subsystem will enable a much faster matching of printing facilities and supplies against publishers' proposals for titles and quantities to be issued in a given year – a task which is at present described as 'a vast arithmetical exercise' which occupies several departments of the State Committee for Publishing for four or five months each year, and even so depends greatly on the use of experience and intuition.[40]

The Soviet book trade network is to employ another subsystem, ASU–PECHAT′–TORG, both as a means of stock control and in order to speed the transmission of pre-publication orders to publishers.[41] Under the present manual system, book trade organisations must submit advance orders to publishers within two-and-a-half months of receiving their publication plans for the coming year. Most of this period is spent in transcribing orders from bookshops into overall orders at district, republic and national level, and it is hoped that this process can be much more highly centralised when the automated subsystem is introduced. The subsystem will also facilitate the allocation of copies to each trading organisation when, as is often the case, the number of advance orders exceeds the number of copies which can be printed. It will also enable the rapid production of book sales analyses, according to publisher, type of work, trading organisation or individual title.

Another subsystem known to be under development, ASU–PECHAT'–BIBLIOGRAF, is to take as input the full bibliographic data for all newly published Soviet books and pamphlets, using for this purpose the 'control copies' deposited at the All-Union Book Chamber (the central Soviet bibliographic registration agency). Besides making these particulars available to other subsystems of ASU–PECHAT' as necessary, this subsystem will be the basis for a range of computer-produced current bibliographies.[42]

The interest of ASU–PECHAT' lies not so much in the specific tasks which it is intended to perform, nor in the computer techniques it employs (insofar as they have been made public), as in the example it offers of the application of large-scale, interlocking subsystems to the planning and recording of an entire nation's book production – from the author's initial proposal through the various stages of editing and production to bibliographic description, the analysis of sales, and the forecasting and (in the Soviet case) regulation of future publications. Several Soviet industries have already experienced considerable difficulties in commissioning large-scale 'automated management systems', and ASU–PECHAT' is unlikely to be a complete exception in this respect; but the effects of the system's limitations on the publishing process should be as interesting to observers as the nature of the demands which the Soviet publishing industry is proposing to make on the system at present envisaged.

5

The publishing-house

As the previous chapters have indicated, the high degree to which Party and state authorities determine the development and operation of Soviet publishing leaves to the individual publishing-house a severely limited number of directions in which it, as an enterprise, can make important decisions between different options. In recent years, some opinion has been expressed in the Soviet Union that central administration of cultural and educational undertakings, including publishing, should be more flexible and imaginative in its relationship to the creative process,[1] and should restrict its regulation to coordinating work, setting the main ideological lines for publishing plans, and specifying the most important topics to be treated;[2] but moves towards allowing the publishing-house greater discretion in economic and editorial matters have, so far at least, changed its situation to a strictly limited extent. This chapter deals with the relationship of a publishing-house to its controlling organisation (since there is no publisher which is not in this very directly subordinate position); the powers and responsibilities of its staff and consultative organs; its economic situation; its selection and handling of manuscripts; salaries and incentives; the decisions made in its internal planning (including the setting of edition sizes); and its links with the censorship.

5.1. *The publishing-house and its superior organisation*

A publishing-house may be subordinated solely and directly to the system of the State Committee for Publishing (either to the union committee, as in the case of most 'central' publishers, or to one of the republic committees, or to an *oblast'* or *krai* publishing administration); it may be under dual subordination and answerable both to a state committee for publishing and to some other organisation or institution (like the Kiev house Radyans'kii Pis'mennik, which is subordinated jointly to the Ukrainian SSR's State Committee for Publishing and to the republic's Writers' Union); or, thirdly, it may

48

be directly administered by a different single organisation, such as the Central Committee of the CPSU (which administers Politizdat) or the Artists' Union (which administers Sovetskii Khudozhnik). In the second and third cases, the USSR State Committee for Publishing retains the power to apply its 'coordination' procedures to all publishers regardless of subordination; to lay down standards and obligatory models for many aspects of their internal functioning; and to determine important factors in their economic performance, such as retail prices, and paper and printing capacity allocations. The 'Statute on the socialist state publishing-house' of 1968 applies to all publishers operating as enterprises on *khozraschet* with the status of juridical persons, and establishes their fundamental ideological, financial and organisational obligations and rights.[3] Despite the statement in the preamble of the 'Statute' that a publishing-house's work is founded on both direction (*rukovodstvo*) from above, and economic independence (*samostoyatel'nost'*) and initiative, the house's economic activity is subject to at least as much control as its editorial choices.

Under the terms of the 'Statute', the publishing-house's superior organ lays down the control figures under which the publisher works in preparing each set of annual plans. These plans, after discussion with appropriate interested organisations, must in their turn be approved by the superior organ, which is responsible for ensuring the finance and supplies to enable their fulfilment. The director of a publishing-house is appointed by the superior organ; and deputy directors, senior editorial staff and the chief accountant are appointed by the superior organ on the director's recommendation. In addition to the superior organ's representation on the house's advisory councils, it is obliged to conduct a thorough review of the house's work annually; and the publisher's performance and methods are permanently subject, like those of other enterprises, to the scrutiny of the Peoples' Control agencies and to the supervision of Party organs described in chapter 3.

5.2. *The director and editorial staff*

The director of a publishing-house is appointed and dismissed by its superior organ and carries full personal responsibility for the house's work, including the ideological and other qualities of all publications issued and the fulfilment of publishing and economic plans. As has been indicated above, many of the most important conditions affecting the house's economic activity are outside his control, although he may now set the house's internal economic indicator figures without outside permission. The publishing plans compiled by him and his staff are subject to approval and amendment by his superiors in the organ controlling the house. In matters of staffing, all regulations for premium payments must be confirmed by the director in agreement with the local trade-union committee, and the dismissal of employees must also have this committee's consent. The director's concern with the content of his house's publications is expected to extend to signing the more important manuscripts before they are passed to the printers, and to discussing with the staff directly involved such matters as edition size, publicity arrangements and the economics of the work.[4]

The publishing-house's chief editor usually acts as first deputy director (the second deputy being in charge of production and supplies). His personal responsibility covers the compilation and fulfilment of the publication plans, and the quality of the books published. He supervises the choice of authors and manuscripts, and is expected to read the more important manuscripts himself.

The editor who is responsible for the handling of a given manuscript (*vedushchii redaktor*) is the publishing-house's chief direct contact with its author. Within the publishing-house, the recommendation to accept or reject each manuscript or author's proposal lies in the first instance with him, though subject to the approval of the head of his editorial office (*zaveduyushchii redaktsiei*) and the chief editor – except, of course, for major works, which will be considered by the house's editorial council, and for material which the house has been instructed to publish by higher authority. Subsequent preparation of the text, consultation with the author over amendments, the book's progress through each stage of production, and the assessment of its reception by the public, are all carried out or supervised by the editor. His duties are explicitly regarded as political, as well as literary and administrative, and he is expected to 'consider each work from the point of view of the Party's and the people's interests'.[5] Where a fundamental difference arises between the senior management and the editor over whether to publish a work, the director is supposed to inform the house's superior organ,[6] but no suggestion has been found that this procedure is resorted to frequently, if at all.

Increasing stress is being laid on the need for editors to become more active in establishing which subjects need to be treated by publication, in attracting authors to write on them, and in participating in the compilation of publication plans. The practice has been widespread among publishers of simply awaiting authors' initiatives in proposing works for publication, and of depending on this so-called 'drift' (*samotek*) to fill their publishing plans.[7] (About 65–70 per cent of the 300 or so titles published annually by Mysl' were originating in authors' proposals in 1973,[8] although Politizdat in 1968 published only 25 per cent of its titles from this source, while 60 per cent were proposed by editorial staff, and 15 per cent were published on the instruction of superior organisations.)[9] Instances have been quoted by Soviet publishers of preparatory work on publication plans beginning at the level of editorial office heads, without involving the editors themselves, who were sometimes not even told the outcome of their recommendations on a manuscript, and were unaware of what manuscripts were awaiting editorial work.[10] Senior editorial staff have also been accused of giving too little attention to the content of some publications. The chairman of the State Committee for Publishing quoted in 1971 a case in which Ekonomika published a work containing many (unspecified) errors. Investigation showed that no-one in the house except the editor dealing directly with the work had read it. At the Progress house, it was found on one occasion that the head of one editorial office had not read a single manuscript included in the year's publication plan.[11]

5.3. *Editorial councils*

All publishing-houses may have attached to them editorial, technical and artistic councils in an advisory capacity, and nearly all houses do in practice make use of such bodies under varying organisations and titles. The editorial council in particular is publicly presented as an important source of advice to the director and his staff, and as a vital link between the publishing-house and the readership which it serves. The council's membership is confirmed by the director in consultation with all interested parties, particularly the house's superior organ; and the director and chief editor act as its chairman and deputy chairman respectively. The publishing-house has an obligation to be guided by (*opirat'sya na*) the recommendations of its editorial council,[12] and is expected to consult it on all important questions of editorial policy, although its resolutions can only be put into effect with the approval of the director. Its

membership will normally include academic and practising specialists in the subjects with which the house deals, senior staff of the
house itself, and representatives of interested organisations, usually
including the Party and government ministries, often the book trade,
and sometimes major libraries. The council considers annual and
longer-term editorial preparation and publishing plans, and proposals for the issue of the more important individual titles and
series. It also studies some works in manuscript, particularly those
which are the subject of conflicting reports from the house's
referees, and those which are the first works of new authors. The
full council is supposed to meet at least once every six months.

Editorial councils vary greatly in size, but those of the major
publishing-houses are often so large (Kolos had about 600 members
in 1974, and Meditsina 279)[13] that a variety of means are used to
enable discussion by smaller groups of council members, which
undertake many of the council's duties. Prosveshchenie, the chief
publisher of Russian-language school textbooks, has an editorial
council attached to each of its twenty editorial offices, with a
presidium of the full council to give approval to overall publication
plans. At Politizdat, the role of an editorial council is taken by the
five subject sections of the house's chief editorial office, which
(unusually) includes a high proportion of non-staff members: of the
twenty-three members of its philosophy section in 1972, only eight
were on the established staff of the house. Others were heads of
department at several higher educational institutions, and staff of
the Institute of Marxism–Leninism and the Academy of Social
Sciences. Members attended section meetings as required by the
subject under discussion, and Politizdat has claimed that the system
has resulted in more active participation by external advisers than
the usual practice under which the editorial council gives its
approval to publishing plans, in the detailed preparation of which
it has taken little part.[14] Some other publishers draw on a wide
range of external consultants in a similar manner.

The transfer of publishing-houses to the new planning and incentive system is said to have intensified the work of many editorial
councils on publishing plans, and to have increased councils' concern with their houses' economic performance. At least one publisher
(Budivel'nik in the Ukraine) has set up a separate economic council,
chaired by the deputy director but consisting largely of external
members, to monitor the house's general economic progress and
advise on economic measures affecting individual titles.[15]

5.4. *The economic position of the publishing-house*

The number of economic planning indicators which have to be laid down annually for a publishing-house by its superior organ was much reduced by new regulations in 1971 which initiated the full-scale transfer of publishing-houses to the new planning and incentive system (applied experimentally to a few publishers from 1969). Under these regulations, instead of 102 such indicators, there are now only nine (ten for publishers making a planned loss), and two more set by the State Committee for Publishing in all cases.[16]

1. Annual plan of titles to be published during the year, to account for at least 80 per cent of planned output expressed in printed sheet-copies, the remainder to be used by the house as a reserve, from which titles will be presented for confirmation during the plan year. This is regarded as the most important indicator, underlying all internal planning as well as contracts with printers and booksellers.

2. Output in printed sheet-copies, with a breakdown at least into output of books, journals, newspapers and graphical publications. State committees for publishing in the republics have the power to specify a breakdown of output in greater detail.

3. Total sales receipts (i.e. at retail prices less discount to the book trade).

4. Planned amount of profit and loss.

5. Amount of payments into, or subventions from, the state budget.

6. Target for reduction of losses (for houses making a planned loss).

7. Funds for salaries and authors' fees.

8. Ceiling for allocation to support central administrative apparatus.

9. Amount of capital investment from central sources.

10. Fixed assets brought into use as a result of capital investment.

11. Allocation of printing capacity.

12. Allocation of paper and binding materials.

Most of these indicators are quite crucially dependent on the amount of paper and printing capacity (indicators 11 and 12) assigned to the publisher through the channels of the State Committee for Publishing regardless of the house's formal subordination. These two will absolutely determine the total output in printed sheet-copies (indicator 2). An advance estimate of them will influence the number of titles included in the publishing plan (indicator 1) and the publisher's proposals for the edition size of each. More indirectly it will influence the selection of titles for publication in order to achieve the best possible economic performance in terms of plan fulfilment within these anticipated limits, while remaining within the house's 'profile' of specialisation and satisfying its superior organ's requirements for subject coverage and ideological emphasis. The combination of indicators 1 and 2 will in turn largely determine total sales receipts (indicator 3), amount of profit or loss (indicator 4), payments into or subventions from the state budget (indicator 5), and, where applicable, the target for loss reduction (indicator 6). Indicator 7 (funds for salaries and authors' fees) also depends on the amount of work handled by the house and the nature of the publications issued, since staff establishments are related by formula to the number of authors' sheets dealt with, and some types of material command lower authors' fees than others – or, where the copyright protection has expired or the book is written in the course of the author's employment, no fees at all.[17]

The reduction in the number of indicators laid down from above did permit publishers somewhat greater flexibility in their internal planning. For instance, they are no longer obliged to seek permission before switching a book's publication date to a different quarter of the plan year. Formerly, if this had been done without an approved reason, the entire staff might have lost part of their incentive payments.[18]

A second important feature of the economic reform as applied to publishing-houses has been the altered conditions for the creation and use of incentive funds. These had previously been calculated as a proportion of over-plan profits. However, publishers were often unable to earn over-plan profits because of paper shortages, and this was said to have prompted them to substitute more profitable titles for those originally included in their publication plans. In the first nine months of 1968, the central publishing-houses fulfilled their profit plans by 127 per cent, making over-plan profits of 13 525 000r., of which 55 per cent was due to changes in the range of publications (*assortimentnyi sdvig*).[19] Under the reformed system, incentive funds are calculated primarily as a proportion of those profits which arise from meeting, rather than surpassing, the plan. Payments into incentive funds from over-plan profits are calculated at a rate at least 30 per cent lower than that applied to planned profits, and payments are made at the full rate only if the publication plan is met. The intention is that profits, or reductions in losses, should be made by more economical use of materials, improved organisation and better labour discipline, rather than by a greater output of books on, say, housekeeping, cookery, fishing and gardening, which have been cited as types of work which are highly profitable and in great demand.[20]

Publishing-houses which have transferred to the new planning and incentive system have emphasised that successful performance and high incentive payments depend on establishing a stable publishing plan of titles which can be reliably expected to appear at the forecast time, and on reducing production costs. These are in turn favoured by the longer planning timetable now being introduced and described in 4.6; by tighter internal control over the movement of manuscripts in the editorial and production stages; and by education of editorial staff in the implications of their work for a book's economic effect on the publishing-house. Systems of 'internal *khozraschet*' are being introduced into many publishing-houses in order to increase awareness of economic considerations. These systems lay down a small number of economic indicators for each editorial office, which are allowed to affect incentive payments and 'socialist competition' results. At Liesma in Riga, these indicators include: deadlines for passing manuscripts to the production department; number of titles and publishers' sheets issued; and expenditure on authors' fees. At the Ekonomika house, each editorial office's expenditure per publisher's sheet is also treated as an indicator.[21]

5.5. Selection and handling of manuscripts

A manuscript submitted to a publishing-house may simply arrive on the author's own initiative (a case of *samotek*). It may have been written under a contract with the publisher which was drawn up on the basis of an outline of the work agreed between author and publisher. Finally, it may be sent by the house's superior organ with instructions to publish. This latter practice appears to be frequently abused, prompting references to persons in authority who exert improper pressure on publishing-houses to accept the work of favoured authors,[22] or who use their position to force a publishing-house to allow them to participate in working on a prestigious book.[23] The chief editor of one publishing-house commented in 1977 that an incompetent writer will usually approach a publisher fully armed with recommendations from departments of the Writers' Union and other influential people, who will lay stress on the topicality of his theme, the years of work he has devoted to it, and the fact that he has published nothing for a long time.[24]

Initiatives by the publishing-house, to secure works on topics which it believes should be treated in print, vary from the informal to the highly institutionalised. Many houses publishing in scholarly fields maintain standing contact with research institutes, and may make agreements with them to publish series of works produced by the institutions' staff. Limitations of this approach are, of course, that the research being undertaken may not correspond to the topics which the publisher is proposing, and that the institutes may be unwilling to prepare the kinds of publication which the publisher believes to be in demand. The publishing-house Yuridicheskaya Literatura contacted its entire list of authors three times, unsuccessfully, in the search for someone to prepare a course on forensic psychology. It also reported that institutions undertaking research in law appeared to have withdrawn entirely from the compilation of collections of legislation on specialised branches of industry, for which the demand was enormous.[25]

In considering an author's proposal for a work, the publishing-house must examine it with the author in detail and agree upon modifications where necessary, a process which is allowed to take up to one-and-a-half months, before notifying him of its rejection or signing a contract for the work to be written.[26] The proposal for any non-fictional work must include a summary or list of chapters which, when agreed with the publisher, forms part of the contract with the author. An accepted proposal must be sent for coordination by the State Committee for Publishing before the contract is signed. The contract must follow the form of approved model contracts (described in 6.2).

An unsolicited manuscript reaching the publishing-house is usually considered initially by the head of the appropriate editorial office or an editor at his direction, and may be sent for refereeing or to other 'appropriate organs' for comment before the decision is made on rejection, modification or acceptance. A manuscript produced under contract will go to the editor in charge of the title, who will likewise study it in detail and take further advice before making a written recommendation about the action to be taken. General requirements affecting manuscripts' suitability stipulate *partiinost'*, high quality of content, and absence of any matter contrary to the interests of a socialist state or to the observance of state secrets. It is no longer obligatory for a publisher to send manuscripts for the opinion of outside referees, except in the case of textbooks, but editors are strongly advised to seek further opinions at this or any other point in working on the manuscript, where such a course might prove of value. The editor's recommendation is considered by a senior editor or the head of his editorial office before being forwarded to the chief editor and director. The decision must be notified to the author within thirty days from receipt of the manuscript, plus four days per author's sheet (extended by any time spent by other 'appropriate organs' in considering it, plus two weeks).[27] If approval (*odobrenie*) is given, and the work is unsolicited, a contract is then signed with the author after the 'coordination' process has been completed.

The approval by the publishing-house of a completed manuscript is regarded as the most crucial action in its handling of the work, since it commits the house, under its contract with the author, not only to paying 60 per cent of the author's fee (less any advance previously made), but – subject to some reservations – to publishing the work within a stipulated time. Approval must be confirmed by the chief editor or director after the editor and the head of the editorial office have made their recommendations. The publishing-house may not reject a manuscript written under contract unless it fails to meet the terms of that contract (for example, as regards length), or unless its contents prove unsuitable in quality or lack *partiinost'*. The courts have no power to adjudicate between publisher and author over rejection of a manuscript on these grounds.[28] The publishing-house may decide, or be instructed, not to publish the work even after it has notified the author of its approval and has paid 60 per cent of the fee. In this situation, a house will frequently refuse to pay the author the balance of the fee that is due to him on publication of the work; but the Supreme Court of the USSR has ruled that, where publication becomes impossible because of altered political circumstances or other reasons not the fault of the author, the house is bound to pay the author's fee in full;[29] and where a refusal has been contested in the courts by the author, payment in full has sometimes, though not always, been ordered. Perhaps the most celebrated of such cases has been that in which the writer Lidiya Chukovskaya successfully claimed the balance of her fee in 1965, after the publishing-house Sovetskii Pisatel' had stopped publication of her previously approved work *Sofiya Petrovna* because of fresh directives to publishers after the Central Committee plenum of October 1964.[30]

Special provisions apply to the acceptance or rejection of a work submitted to a publisher by an institute of the USSR Academy of Sciences. If a publishing-house disagrees with 'positions' adopted in the text of such a work, it must state its objections to the director of the institute. The director may then, if he so decides, confirm his institution's approval of the work by signing it a second time, in which case the publisher will print it as submitted, but responsibility for any consequences will lie exclusively with the author and the institute director.[31]

A publishing-house may not alter or shorten a manuscript without the author's permission, and the author has the right to object to proposals for such alterations, provided that his own preferred text is well grounded in scholarship and does not conflict with the interests of a socialist state, the principle of *partiinost'*, or the preservation of official secrets. Any addition by the publisher of an introduction or notes may likewise be made only with the author's permission.[32] This qualified freedom of the author to adhere to his own views attracted some interest as an innovation when it was introduced in the 1967 instructions for manuscript preparation.[33] If the disagreement between author and editor cannot be resolved, the house's editorial council is consulted, after which the publishing-house director either decides in favour of the author, or, if the latter persists in refusing the proposed amendments, terminates the contract.

The editor preparing an accepted manuscript for publication is responsible for establishing the presence of any information not intended for open publication. (This requirement implies some liaison between editorial staff and the censorship, even if indirect.) Any alteration or excision arising from this examination must be agreed with the author and with any external editor being consulted over the manuscript, who must both sign a corrected copy.[34] Other editorial work will include stylistic polish, the checking of references and citations, consideration of any external editors' and referees' reports, and in some cases further discussion within the editorial office or with the chief editor, before the complete manuscript is sent for re-reading (*vychitka*), or is re-read in full by the editor himself. Any further corrections as a result of the re-reading must again be made in agreement with the author, and the resulting manuscript is expected to be in every respect ready for the compositor. It is then signed by the editor, the head of the editorial office, the chief editor, and – for important works – by the director, before being sent to the production department, where its movement is expected to be in accordance with a centrally approved set of flow charts.

5.6. *Salaries and incentives*

Salary scales for publishing-house staff are laid down centrally, although the director of a house, in agreement with the local trade-union committee, has limited discretion in their application to his own enterprise. He may, for example, increase salaries by up to 30 per cent for especially highly qualified staff, and with the consent of the house's superior organ may draw on up to 0.3 per cent of the salary fund for this purpose. Over the use of the house's incentive funds, though not the principles of their formation, he has somewhat more freedom of action, though again in agreement with the trade-union committee.[35] Personal responsibility for keeping outlay on salaries within the limits of the salary fund extends to the director and chief editor, their deputies, the chief accountant and departmental heads, all of whom are liable to the total or partial loss of their incentive payments if held to be at fault in this respect. The State Bank (Gosbank) has an important role in supervising the use of salary funds by enterprises, since it permits their accounts to be drawn on for this purpose only in accordance with the expenditure plans compulsorily notified to it.

Basic salary scales (before incentive additions) for administrative and editorial staff vary according to the type of publishing-house.[36] Since 1976, the salaries of staff in 'leading' central book publishing-houses have been on the same level as those for staff of central daily newspapers, with staff of 'other' central houses receiving slightly less. (The list of central book publishers regarded as 'leading' was not available at the time of writing, but the salary scales previously in force gave preferential treatment to staff of Politizdat, Atomizdat, Vneshtorgizdat, Mysl', Ekonomika, Progress, Mir, Sovetskaya Entsiklopediya, Statistika, APN, and the chief editorial office of the Ukrainian Soviet Encyclopedia, presumably because in these cases a need had been conceded to attract staff of especially high calibre.)[37] Salaries of staff in non-central publishing-houses have been fixed between 10 and 25 per cent lower than those of local newspaper staff at equivalent levels, though no justification for this lack of comparability has been found. Publishing staff with a higher university degree, working in a capacity which requires their special knowledge, are paid on the scales of senior staff in scientific research institutions. In 1975, a chief editor with a candidate's degree at a central publishing-house was said to be earning about 400r. per month, and a senior scientific editor about 340r.[38]

The formation of incentive funds, under the new planning and incentive system, is regulated by the State Committee for Publishing in agreement with Gosplan.[39] Three such funds are now maintained by all publishers on the new system: the material incentive fund (for the payment of premia based on plan fulfilment, special payments to individuals for contributions to the issue of important works, and grants for assistance in cases of special need); the social, cultural and accommodation fund (for living accommodation and recreational facilities); and the publishing technology fund (intended for additional equipment, vehicles, etc.). The income of all three funds comes from the house's profits (or reduced losses) at rates approved by the State Committee for Publishing. In the case of the publishing technology fund, extra income is derived as a percentage deduction from depreciation allowances and from the sale of unwanted equipment. Formulae for calculating rates of payment into the first two funds are at present (1977) required to depend to between 70 and 90 per cent on the achievement of planned sales, and to between 10 and 30 per cent on the amount of profit, or reduction in losses. Payments to incentive funds are also conditional upon the house's issuing the number of titles included in the publishing plan, and on achieving the planned output in printed sheet-copies of the different types of publication which it issues.

Sales and profits above the planned levels permit further payments to the incentive funds, but at a rate at least 30 per cent lower than that fixed for the planned levels. Where plans are not fulfilled, payments to the incentive funds are reduced in proportion to the degree of non-fulfilment, but at rates raised by at least 30 per cent. Up to half the reduction may be remitted if the shortfall is made good in the following plan quarter. Where plan targets have had to be reduced because of paper shortages, the State Committee for Publishing may waive the payment rules applied to reduced performance.

A central reserve incentive fund is maintained by the State Committee for Publishing, formed from a 5 per cent deduction from the incentive funds of all its publishing-houses. This is used to increase the incentive funds of publishers as a reward for special achievements, such as increasing export sales, saving paper, and applying new techniques.[40]

Premia paid to staff from the material incentive fund are made under principles agreed between the State Committee for Publishing and the State Committee for Labour and Wages.[41] Conditions for the award of premia to managing staff (the director and chief editor, their deputies, the head of the planning department and the chief accountant) must be set by the house's superior organ, and must include the achievement of sales and profit targets by the publishing-house as a whole, fulfilment of the publication and total output plans, and high quality in the books issued. Conditions for the award of premia to the other staff are set by the house's management in agreement with the trade-union committee. For editorial staff, obligatory conditions are high quality of work, the maintenance of schedules in handling manuscripts, and meeting the publishing-house's obligations to printers and booksellers over timetables and deliveries. Where editorial offices are operating on internal *khozraschet*, their obligatory conditions also include meeting sales and profit targets. Premia paid to managing staff must not be higher than the average percentage paid to other employees. An individual's premia may be increased or lowered by up to 25 per cent in recognition of his contribution (or lack of it) to his department's work; and premia may be refused entirely to staff who are held responsible for publications unsatisfactory in quality or content, for not meeting production schedules, breach of contractual requirements, or absenteeism.

In practice, premia are usually distributed on a fairly undifferentiated basis: at the Ekonomika house in 1973, over half the material incentive fund was allocated at a more or less equal rate among all the staff for quarterly plan results, and increases or reductions were rarely more than 10 per cent.[42] It has been calculated that, as a result of the introduction of the new incentive system, payments per publishing-house employee from the incentive funds rose from an average 184r. annually in 1968 to 373r. in 1972.[43] Average additional earnings from incentives for staff of central scientific and technical publishers was estimated at about 400r. annually in 1974.[44] By 1975, material incentive funds in some publishing-houses had risen well above the norm of 22 per cent of the house's salary fund: to 28.4 per cent in Estonia, 32.2 per cent in the Ukraine, and 38.4 per cent in Belorussia.[45] This rapid growth in incentive funds (not only in publishing, but throughout the economy) has more recently been slowed down by administrative action. Since 1976, incentive funds have not been allowed to grow at a faster rate than profits, and for 1977 the Ministry of Finance and Gosplan stipulated that enterprises' incentive funds should remain at the same level as in 1976, regardless of any increase in sales or profits.[46]

A further incentive is provided by 'socialist competition', in which performance is likewise judged on plan fulfilment and quality of books issued, and rewards are drawn from over-plan profits and (where necessary) the 'free remainder' of planned profits (i.e. those not put back into the enterprise and therefore payable to the state budget). Prizes and bonuses in competitions between publishers are adjudged by the union or republic state committees for publishing. Many houses have introduced 'internal socialist competition' between their departments, into which a variety of criteria have been introduced to improve different aspects of the house's performance, such as the adoption of high individual counter-plans and progress in raising qualifications.

5.7. *Internal planning decisions*

Planning work within a publishing-house includes preparation of the annual and longer-term plans of titles to be issued, and of the editorial preparation plans which underpin them; planning the movements of manuscripts and printed sheets through the processes of production and distribution in collaboration with printers and book trade organs; and the administrative and economic planning designed to ensure the correct amount and variety of supplies and staff and to obtain the economic results stipulated by the house's superior organ. The publishing-house's planning department, or, in smaller enterprises, economists immediately subordinated to the director, undertakes the detailed work of relating the editorial and publishing plans (drafted by the editorial staff) to the superior organ's control figures and allocated paper and printing resources. The department calculates the economic prospects of each title; prepares the house's financial plan; monitors progress towards meeting all planning objectives; records the movement of all manuscripts; calculates retail prices and staff establishment according to the approved tables and standards for the director's confirmation; and supplies analyses of performance and such other management information as is required.[47]

Although the publishing-house as a whole, and often each editorial office within it, will have strict limits on paper and printing facilities, the choice of titles to include in the publishing plans begins with the selection decisions accepting authors' proposals, commissioning the writing of works, and approving submitted manuscripts. It is from this reservoir of the 'contract portfolio' and the 'editorial portfolio' (works in preparation or on the premises in manuscript form)[48] that the editorial preparation plans and publication plans are compiled – including, of course, any material which the publishing-house may be instructed to issue by its superior organ. Although some publishers have stressed that planning normally begins in this way, 'from the bottom', with the selection of manuscripts, while the economic prospects of each title remain a secondary consideration,[49] it is clear that there is a concurrent responsibility on, and incentives for, the publishing-house management to compile a publication plan which can be adhered to, and a financial plan which can be fulfilled with credit. The difficulties attending the judgment, calculations and experience applied to the publishing plan are shown by the extent to which some publishers in the event fail to meet that plan. In 1973, the degree of fulfilment (*real'nost'*) of the publishing plan for Voenizdat was 67 per cent, and for Sovetskaya Rossiya only 54 per cent.[50] In some of the peripheral republics plan fulfilment is even lower: of the 439 titles planned for publication by Azerbaidzhan publishers between 1974 and mid-1976, only 155 had appeared by late 1976.[51]

5.8. *Edition sizes*

The edition size (*tirazh*) of a book is one of the most significant features in its unit production cost, and is also regarded in the USSR as one of the determinants, along with the work's quality, of its social impact. The effect of edition size on unit cost, and hence on profit, is shown in table 2, which illustrates how a work issued in 15 000 copies may make a loss of 6740r., while 75 000 copies of the same work would bring the publisher a profit of 4073r.

Although publishers make a preliminary estimate of the edition size for each title when preparing their annual publishing plan, they are usually strongly influenced in the number of copies which they finally order from the printer by the number of copies which the book trade organisations order in advance of publication. Formally, the size of the edition is set jointly (*sovmestno*) by the publisher and the bookselling organisations,[52] as is the size of any reissue – a situation which has caused complaints that responsibility for the accuracy of the figure decided upon is unclear. The greater share of the responsibility appears to lie with the publishing-house, since under other instructions its director has the duty to establish (*ustanavlivat'*) the edition size, and the house has the right to increase the number of copies, at its own financial risk, beyond the amount ordered by the book trade, or to exclude a title from its

Table 2. *Effect of edition size on unit cost*

	Variant 1	Variant 2
Size of work in publisher's sheets	19.92	19.92
Edition size	15 000	75 000
Publisher's sheet-copies	298 800	1 494 000
Retail earnings at 88k. per copy	13 200r.	66 000r.
Publisher's receipts at 75% of retail earnings	9 900r.	49 500r.
Publisher's costs		
Author's fee	7 077r.	13 701r.
Editorial costs at 104r. per sheet	2 072r.	2 072r.
General overheads at 40r. per sheet	796r.	796r.
Printing charges	2 195r.	6 460r.
Paper	1 875r.	9 375r.
Binding: materials and labour	2 308r.	11 438r.
Incidental (*vneproizvodstvennye*) costs at 2.4% of retail earnings	317r.	1 585r.
Total	16 640r.	45 427r.
Profit/loss	−6 740r.	+4 073r.

Source
V. Marshak, 'Tsena, sebestoimost', pribyl'', *V mire knig*, 1975(9), 25–6.

publishing plan if too few orders are received.[53] On occasions, and more frequently now that greater stress is being laid on profitability, a publishing-house may resort to simple publicity measures to increase the number of orders for books in their plan which would otherwise make a loss. Mysl', for example, has found it possible to triple and even quintuple the number of orders for a book by circulating a few hundred brochures to interested organisations. Another cause of an increased edition size is a favourable review, or preview, in an authoritative publication, which may be sufficient to secure an additional allocation of paper. A review in *Pravda* of the book *Sovetsko-kitaiskie otnosheniya 1945–1970* (*Soviet–Chinese relations 1945–1970*) by O. B. Borisov and B. T. Koloskov, published by Mysl' in 1971, made it possible to raise the edition size from 13 000 (planned on the basis of pre-publication orders) to 40 000.[54]

Agreement between the publisher and the bookselling organisations over the edition size may be reached either informally or (sometimes only in the case of a disagreement) through the machinery of a commission (*tirazhnaya komissiya*), composed of representatives of the publishing-house, bookselling organisations, and other bodies including the republic or union State Committee for Publishing. Central publishing-houses often have such a commission attached to their enterprise exclusively, while the peripheral republics and *oblasti* have commissions dealing with edition sizes in all publishers in their area. Disagreements within a commission, usually as a result of booksellers' requesting more copies of a popular work than the publishers' paper allocation allows them to print, are ruled upon by the appropriate State Committee for Publishing.[55]

5.9. Censorship

The main organ of censorship in the USSR is the Chief Administration for the Protection of State Secrets in the Press attached to the Council of Ministers of the USSR, usually – and quite often in print – referred to as Glavlit. It is distinct from the specialised censorships applied to material dealing with, for example, military matters, atomic energy, space technology and state security. In most cases the approval of the specialised censorship offices must be obtained before the material is passed by the publishing-house to the Glavlit censors, but the state security (KGB) censorship is consulted only through Glavlit.[56] Glavlit's approval (indicated usually by a serial number printed at the end of the book) is required for the publication of almost all printed matter. The number is omitted from the national bibliographical publications and from some Party and government documents (leaders' speeches, Central Committee and Party Congress reports, the journal *Vedomosti* of union and republic supreme soviets, and the union and republic journals

Sobraniya postanovlenii pravitel'stva); and from editions of the works of Marx, Engels and Lenin. The censor's serial number is also omitted from translations of foreign fiction published in the USSR, possibly because the stringent regulations applying to the selection of works for translation (described in 9.9) is deemed an adequate safeguard.[57] The fact that works for distribution outside the Soviet Union do not show the censor's serial number is most unlikely to indicate that they are exempt from censorship.

State secrets are protected under articles 64, 65, 75, 76 and 259 of the RSFSR Criminal Code. Glavlit is believed to take its direct authority from a decree of the USSR Council of Ministers of 1956,[58] which in its public form lists in general terms matters of military, economic and political importance which rank as state secrets (military plans and information, strategic industries, mineral resources, codes, currency reserves, important inventions), and possibly also from other, unpublished legislation. It is an all-union organisation, and most of the detailed censorship is carried out by Glavlit staff permanently accommodated on the premises of each publishing-house.[59] Publications issued by bodies which are not themselves publishing-houses are subject not only to Glavlit's censorship but to its approval of the distribution of copies of each title.[60] Glavlit sanction was also required for the list currently in force of types of printed matter which may be issued free of charge by specified organisations.[61]

The accounts of former Soviet authors and editors state that Glavlit censorship is not applied to works in manuscript unless the publisher specifically requests advice about material before it is sent to the compositor *(sdano v nabor),*[62] or unless Glavlit itself asks to see a manuscript about which it has apprehensions.[63] The galley-proofs *(granki)* as corrected by author and editor must be censored in detail, both for the mention of prohibited topics and for the observance of political lines and nuances, before they can be 'signed for the press' *(podpisano v pechat').* It has been claimed that Glavlit cannot formally forbid a work's publication unless a state secret has been disclosed. If a publisher insists on a text which the censor considers undesirable for reasons other than state secrecy, the censorship can only make a report to the Central Committee.[64] (In a reported recent case, the publisher Iskusstvo ignored 'advice' not to publish I. V. Ivanov's book on the Czech theatrical figure Jan Werich. The work was removed from circulation shortly after publication by an order of the State Committee for Publishing, the editor who handled it was dismissed, and the director of Iskusstvo severely reprimanded.)[65] Finally, 'signal copies' (*signal'nye ekzemplyary*) of the finished work, run off before the main printing begins, must again be approved by the censor, after any corrections by the editorial staff, before permission is given for publication (*vypusk v svet*).

It seems clear, from the accounts of those who have worked in Soviet publishing, and from the duties of an editor described earlier in this chapter, that part of an editor's responsibility is to apply a form of 'pre-censorship' to manuscripts reaching a publishing-house, if necessary to the extent of rejecting them, before they reach the Glavlit representative. This is said to be particularly common in the case of highly specialised scholarly works, where the Glavlit censors lack the subject knowledge to make an informed check of the contents, and editorial staff are (perhaps tacitly) entrusted with informal censorship duties.[66]

6

The author

The place of the author in Soviet publishing policy is determined by his status as the creator (or compiler, or editor) of publishable material; and by the fact of his being, not part of an enterprise or industry with which publishing – as itself an industry – can conduct relations on the usual inter-sector plane, but one of thousands of individuals at work on books, very many of whom are not full-time writers, and who, even in their capacity as writers, can be institutionalised to only a limited degree. In its concern with the author, Soviet publishing policy bears upon the rights and responsibilities attaching to him as the creator of a manuscript; on the nature of the state's interest in the manuscript itself and its powers with regard to it; on regulation of the author's relationship (contractual and otherwise) with the publishing-house; on regulation of fees paid to the author; and on the position and influence accorded to writers' organisations.

6.1. *The author's rights*

The author's general rights (*avtorskoe pravo*, a term of wider application than 'copyright') are deemed in the Soviet Union to be a matter of civil law. They are specified in outline in the USSR's fundamentals of civil legislation,[1] and in expanded form in the civil codes and other legislation of the constituent republics.[2] Like other civil rights in the USSR, they may be exercised only 'in conformity with their purpose in a socialist society in the period of building communism'.[3] Certain rights attach to the author simply by the fact of his authorship and irrespective of the nature and quality of his work: notably his right to be acknowledged as the author and his right to protection against the use of the work without his permission, with certain reservations. Although these rights normally attach only to individuals (that is, to the author himself and to his heirs for the duration of certain rights after his death), corporate bodies may be granted author's rights in respect of publications of collective authorship issued by them: for example, the TASS news agency, and publishers of collected articles, journals and encyclopedias, though only for each publication as a whole, not for separate authors' identifiable contributions.

It is explicitly acknowledged that even authors of works regarded as injurious to society have the right to recognition as author and the right to protection against unauthorised use, although the works may not be published in the Soviet Union. This latter reservation arises from the qualifications to a further right of the author: to the 'publication, reproduction and distribution[4] of his work by any means allowed by law'.[5] Published Soviet legal opinion is unanimous that this right can be exercised only through a 'socialist organisation' such as a publishing-house, which has the right of selection and rejection. It is further held (though on very ill-defined grounds) that the publication of a book lies outside the legal capacity (*pravosposobnost'*) of an individual citizen;[6] and this view is no doubt at the root of the concept of the 'right to publish', regarded as a privilege conferrable by the Party and state which is in practice granted only to approved organisations.

The author's right to protection against the use of his work in manuscript without his permission is qualified by the provision for the right to publication to be compulsorily purchased by the state on the decision of the appropriate republic's council of ministers. This power is said to be exercised most frequently over an author's heirs, if they oppose the publication of his manuscripts or demand an exorbitant amount for such publication.[7] A related provision allows a work to be declared state property even after the period of protection against unpermitted use has expired, in order to allow the state to restrict, or to supervise more closely, the conditions of its publication.[8] The use of a work without the author's permission *after* publication is additionally allowed (in provisions more broadly framed than those contained in most Western copyright legislation) for purposes of quotation in scientific, critical, educational and political instruction works, within limits corresponding to the purpose of the work and not at greater length than one author's sheet; and for scientific and educational purposes where no profit is made.[9]

6.2. *Contracts between author and publishing-house*

The contracts regulating the relationship between author and publishing-house must conform to models approved by the State

Committee for Publishing. Under the standard form of contract between a Soviet publisher and a Soviet citizen for the first edition of his work,[10] the author agrees not to transmit the work to any other organisation for publication without the first publisher's consent, for a period of three years from the latter's approving the manuscript, except that he may have it, or parts of it, published in newspapers, journals or the *Roman-gazeta* series, provided the contracting publisher is notified. This freedom to re-publish in periodicals is not normal in Western copyright law.

The publishing-house, for its part, is obliged to publish the work within one year from approving it, if it contains up to ten author's sheets, or within two years if it is larger. If the work is not issued within these time limits, the author is entitled to demand the full fee stipulated in the contract, and to require the return of the manuscript unless it has already been signed for printing. In practice, authors are usually willing to allow the publisher much longer delays – often as much as three or four years between approval and publication – rather than exercise their right to have the manuscript returned, probably because the high degree of specialisation among Soviet publishing-houses makes multiple submissions of a manuscript unrewarding. For the period of the contract, the publishing-house has complete discretion, vis-à-vis the author, over the number of copies in which the book is issued, provided that the appropriate fee is paid for works where this is related to the edition size. If an unchanged reissue is proposed by the publisher after the term of the original contract has expired, a new contract covering the reissue must be concluded; and if the reissue is to contain any significant alterations a new contract must be signed even if the original is still in force.

Under a new clause inserted in the model contract approved in 1975, as a consequence of the USSR's adherence to the Universal Copyright Convention in 1973, the author assigns to the publishing-house his powers (*pravomochiya*) over the use of the work abroad, unless they have already been assigned to some other body. The publishing-house agrees to inform the author of any proposals for such use abroad, to safeguard the author's interests in any transaction it may undertake in this connection, and to give him the opportunity to amend or make additions to his work. Unlike the other rights granted by the author under the contract, the powers over the use of the work abroad remain with the publisher for the entire period, extending up to twenty-five years after the author's death, during which time the use of the work is protected by author's rights.

The author agrees under the contract to make alterations or corrections proposed by the publishing-house if such changes would enable an otherwise approved manuscript to be published, and if they arise from circumstances independent of the contracting parties (such as new legislation or more recent statistics); while the publishing-house agrees to make no changes, nor to add illustrations, introductions or notes, without the author's permission. Some Soviet opinion has been expressed that these conditions in the contract prevent the publishing-house editor from exercising the 'guiding influence' on the literary process which is said to be one of his functions, since the author is entitled to turn down the editor's suggestions, other than those which the contract obliges him to accept, provided that the work otherwise complies with the conditions of the contract.[11]

As might be expected, disputes arise over the interpretation of these conditions. For example, one author whose novel had been approved by a publishing-house was subsequently asked to make alterations and deletions because of critics' comments after he (quite legally) published the work in a journal. He turned down the demand, claiming that it was outside the conditions of his contract, but the house then refused to publish the novel.[12] In another case, a translator had his contract terminated by the publisher when he refused to shorten the original work and provide notes to it. In this instance the court awarded the translator the full fee payable for the original length of the work.[13] Such disputes are normally considered by the house's editorial council at the director's request, before he reaches a decision which may be challenged in the courts.

There is evidence, nevertheless, that at least some editors are prepared to demand, and some authors to consent to, very drastic alterations in even a short manuscript. E. Bartenev's book *Taina bytiya cheloveka* (*Secrets of man's existence*), published by Politizdat in 1969, and subsequently described as one of the best in the series in which it appeared, was revised three times by the author, who then rewrote several chapters at the editor's request while the manuscript was being prepared for publication.[14] For this he would have received the standard fee for that type and length of work: between approximately 1200r. and 3600r., depending on the scale applied.[15]

The publisher may terminate the contract, and demand the return by the author of any advance paid, if he can be shown to have acted in bad faith in preparing the work. As examples of bad faith have been quoted plagiarism, distortion in translation, and failure to check statements which required verification. This last obligation is emphasised by the regulations for manuscript preparation, which lay down that the sources of all factual statements and quotations shall be stated by the author (where not cited in his text) on the second copy of his manuscript or in a separate list.

Where the cost of alterations made by the author to proofs exceeds 10 per cent of the composing costs, the amount by which it exceeds that figure will under the contract be deducted from the author's fee. In an effort to reduce the cost of such alterations, this percentage is to be reduced in stages to 3 per cent by 1980, except for encyclopedia contributions, for which the present 30 per cent will fall to 20 per cent. The norms for proof alteration allowed to editorial staff will be similarly reduced over the same period.[16]

6.3. *Authors' fees*

The Soviet author's right to receive a fee for the publication of his work in most circumstances is regarded as his basic property right in the work; but, as in Western publishing, the fee is paid by the publishing-house for the *right to use* the work, not as a direct remuneration to the author for his efforts in completing the manuscript. Payment of the fee is not conditional upon the number of copies sold (as is usual under the Western royalty system), nor upon the publisher's making a profit on the work – although some Soviet publishers have been alleged to illegally refuse fees to authors of scholarly works unless or until they become profitable.[17] Authors' fees are paid according to scales approved by the council of ministers in each union republic (RSFSR scales are shown in appendix 1). Variation between the republics is still considerable, despite a decree of the USSR Council of Ministers in 1968 which imposed a degree of uniformity on the republics' scales for fiction, but allowed them to retain any scales with higher maxima which were already in force.

Common to all the republics' fee scales is the principle of payment, firstly, according to the type of work; and, within the scales set for that, within fixed limits per author's sheet (40 000 typographical units of text). Shorter works may receive a lump-sum payment. For most types of fiction, in the RSFSR scales, a standard edition size (*norma tirazha*) is set, with separate standards for 'ordinary' and 'mass' publications. If a work is published in an edition size larger than the applicable standard, the author receives the fee appropriate for one or more reissues as well as that for the first impression: 60 per cent of the original fee for the second and third issues, 40 per cent for the fourth, 35 per cent for the fifth, and 30 per cent for all subsequent issues. The standard edition sizes for fiction vary from 10 000 to 50 000 copies for 'ordinary' editions, and from 25 000 to 150 000 for 'mass' editions. Fees for non-fiction publications are related to edition size in a different way: authors of mass political and popular scientific literature receive a 50 per cent addition to their fee if the edition size is over 100 000, and a 75 per cent addition if over 200 000. Other non-fiction monographs receive the 50 and 75 per cent additions above 50 000 and 100 000 copies respectively, and textbooks receive an additional 50 per cent for more than 750 000 copies.

RSFSR fee scales for prose fiction are 150–400r. per author's sheet for ordinary, and 250–400r. per sheet for mass editions. Mass political literature is paid at 150–300r. per sheet; most scholarly monographs at the same rate; popular scientific literature at 100–300r. per sheet; course textbooks (*uchebniki*) for higher education and Party instruction in Marxism–Leninism at 150–200r. per sheet; and for schools at 100–200r. per sheet. For mass political literature, the full fee per author's sheet is paid only for the first five sheets, and for popular scientific literature for the first ten: any further length receives only 25 per cent of the basic fee per sheet. Particularly high-quality pamphlets of up to four sheets on social and political subjects may receive a lump sum of up to 1600r. It is worth noting that, with some exceptions, the maximum and minimum of the scale for a given type of work are further apart than the highest and lowest maxima or minima of the scales as a whole. The scales thus allow wide scope for the remuneration of high quality in most types of work, but show less marked differentiation (or priorities) between types of work.

The publishing-house has discretion to negotiate the exact fee per sheet with the author, at one of several points within the limits of the applicable scale, and publishers' policies vary in this matter. Cases have been quoted of a publishing-house which always paid the lowest fees allowed because it was making a planned loss, and consequently drove local authors to other houses; and of a central (unnamed) publishing-house which paid only the highest permissible fees in order to attract authors and give the house a wide choice of manuscripts. A third house created difficulties for itself by habitually paying fees at the middle of the scale to members of the Writers' Union and Journalists' Union, but the lowest possible fees to all other authors. When it was offered a work by two authors, only *one* of whom was a union member, the house felt unable to put two different fee levels (225r. and 150r. per sheet) on the contract, so offered both authors an 'average' of 175r. The authors refused the offer and had the work accepted by another publisher, who gave them 300r. per sheet and published the work in a mass edition with a reissue.[18]

Payment of fees is made in up to three stages. An author contracting to write a work of fiction must receive (in the RSFSR) an advance of 25 per cent of the fee at the scale agreed in the contract. For a non-fictional work he *may* be paid an advance, with the publisher's consent, of up to 25 per cent, but only at the minimum scale for the type of work being written, regardless of the scale actually agreed in the contract. Many publishing-houses prefer not to pay advances unless they are legally obliged to do so, since if the completed manuscript is later rejected as unsuitable for publication, the house can only recover the advance if the author can be shown to have acted in bad faith.[19] Sixty per cent of the fee (less any advance) is then paid when the completed manuscript is approved by the publisher; and the balance, including any additional amount for an edition size above the standard, either after the final sheet of proofs has been signed for printing (in the case of works of fiction), or after the work has been approved for public distribution (*vypusk v svet*). This difference in treatment between fiction and non-fiction may be in order to allow the maximum time for reconsideration of the latter before payment is finally made.

Income tax paid by a Soviet author on fees for work published in the USSR is, like other Soviet income tax, light by Western standards. At the highest rate, on annual earnings from fees of 1201r. and over, he pays 98.40r. plus 13 per cent of the amount exceeding 1200r.[20] However, all income from writing, however small, is subject to tax, whereas salaries are tax-free up to 60 or 70r. per month. While works written by an author in the course of his employment do not normally receive a fee, an important exception applies to all educational textbooks. Fees for these are paid regardless of the conditions under which they were prepared, provided that the book has been commissioned and approved by an education ministry.

There have been repeated claims that the fee scales in some republics give rise to unjustifiably high payments to authors, and hence to inflated production costs for their books, chiefly through lower standard edition sizes for fiction. For example, the standard 'ordinary' and 'mass' edition sizes for prose fiction in the Georgian SSR are 10 000 and 40–50 000 respectively, compared with 15 000 and 50–100 000 in the RSFSR. The result is that a Georgian novel in an edition of 30 000 earns a fee of 220 per cent of the rate for the 'ordinary' standard edition size: 100 per cent plus 60 per cent each for the second and third 'issues'.[21] The reason for these lower standard edition sizes is probably the smaller size of the market, particularly for works in languages other than Russian. They are said to be responsible for the significantly higher proportion formed by authors' fees in the total production cost of books in some republics. In 1972, 19.6 per cent of book production costs were consumed by authors' fees in the Azerbaidzhan SSR, 21.7 per cent in the Armenian SSR, and 26.1 per cent in the Georgian SSR, compared with an all-union average (for publishers at republic level) of 13.7 per cent.[22]

The present practice of fixing authors' fees according to the length of the work, although with disincentives now applied to over-long manuscripts for certain types of publication, has been criticised on occasions at least since the 1950s.[23] Some opinion has been expressed that Soviet authors should have a direct financial interest in the saleability of their work, presumably through some variant of the Western royalty system.[24] The present Soviet fee system probably survives not because the principle of payment by length is positively approved of, but because the implications of payment according to sales are felt to be at variance with central control of publishing policy, and payment according to 'quality' alone would be difficult to apply consistently.

6.4. *The author, translation and publication abroad*

The right of 'freedom of translation' in Soviet law, which permitted any Soviet work to be translated from any one language of the USSR into any other, without the author's permission or the payment of any fee, was modified in 1960 to require payment for translations of fiction into Russian from other languages of the USSR.

It was modified further in 1968 to require a fee for translation of fiction from and into any national language; but for translations of non-fiction the law demanded only that the author be notified immediately after the translation had been approved. 'Freedom of translation' was removed altogether after the USSR adhered to the Universal Copyright Convention in 1973; and no translation for purposes of publication may now be undertaken without the agreement of the author or of those to whom he has assigned his right (*pravopreemniki*) in this matter.[25] Fees are now payable to the author for the publication of his work in translation in most circumstances. In the RSFSR the fees are:

For fiction:

From any USSR language except Russian into any RSFSR language: 60 per cent of the fee applicable to the original.

From Russian into any RSFSR language: 60 per cent of the minimum scale fee.

From any language into any foreign language: 30 per cent of the fee applicable to the original.

For non-fiction: 30 per cent of the fee applicable to the original.[26]

Adherence to the Universal Copyright Convention prompted the Soviet Union to set up the All-Union Agency for Authors' Rights (Vsesoyuznoe agentstvo po avtorskim pravam, or VAAP), which replaced the All-Union Administration for the Defence of Authors' Rights (VUOAP) of the Writers' Union and the corresponding administration of the Artists' Union. VAAP's mandate was extended to enable it to act on behalf of all Soviet writers and other creative artists in negotiating the sale of rights to use their work abroad, and on behalf of all foreign authors whose work is to be published in the USSR.[27] It also advises and represents authors in disputes over their rights within the Soviet Union, supporting them in court actions if it sees fit.[28] The agency has the status of a public body, nominally distinct from any government department and headed by a council representing the founding institutions, which include the State Committee for Publishing, the Writers' Union and the Union of Journalists. The council, which is chaired by the chairman of the State Committee for Publishing, chooses the agency's board of management.

The chief significance of VAAP for the Soviet author wishing to publish abroad is that the right to use his work outside the USSR may only be granted by him (or by a publisher acting on his behalf) under a contract agreed with VAAP, otherwise Soviet law will not recognise the foreign party as a legal recipient of that right.[29] The 1975 model author's contract, as we have seen, gives the author's Soviet publisher the right to negotiate for the use of his work abroad. This contract was complemented by a new type of 'licensing contract' (*litsenzionnyi dogovor*), approved at the same time, which can be used by a publisher undertaking such negotiations in conjunction with VAAP, and simply grants an organisation the right to publish the work of a Soviet author in translation, or the work of a foreign author in the USSR, for a specified period in return for a stated fee. These licensing contracts contrast with the normal contract governing the issue of a Soviet author's work by a Soviet publisher in the USSR, in being examples (*primernye formy*), not obligatory (*tipovye*) models.[30] Divergence from them is permitted in the interests of greater freedom of negotiation, provided that there is no infringement of the law, and that neither party's position is adversely affected.

Representatives of VAAP have stated that they would regard the transfer of a Soviet author's rights abroad, or the obtaining of a foreign author's rights from abroad, other than through VAAP, as a contravention of the foreign trade monopoly granted to VAAP for this kind of traffic.[31] The USSR Supreme Court has ruled that, where an author is found to have sent a work for use abroad with intentions consciously contrary to the interests of a socialist state and society, a court may confiscate any proceeds from the transaction.[32] The author may well also be liable to criminal prosecution for anti-Soviet propaganda, or for defaming the Soviet state and social order.[33]

A Soviet author is entitled to receive payment for the use of his work abroad even if he received no fee for its publication in the USSR – as, for example, where it was written in the course of his employment. All fees received from abroad, however, are subject to Soviet income tax at a much higher rate than that levied on fees paid by Soviet publishers for works published in the USSR. These higher tax rates, introduced in 1973, begin at 30 per cent for sums of up to 500r., while on amounts of 5001r. and over the tax is 2775r. plus 75 per cent of the sum by which the amount exceeds 5000r.[34] VAAP is responsible for the calculation and deduction of this tax, together with its own commission, which is 10 per cent of fees paid to foreign authors for publication of their work in the USSR, and as much as 25 per cent of amounts sent to Soviet authors from foreign countries.[35] The justification claimed for the high tax rates is that the state must use them to obtain compensation for the foreign currency spent by Soviet publishers in paying for rights to use foreign works.

6.5. *The Writers' Union*

Soviet authors (taking as a single body those who write published works on whatever subject) have not proved greatly more apt to institutionalisation in a socialist country than writers elsewhere, although many writers of imaginative literature are members of the Writers' Union of the USSR and its daughter unions in the republics, and a smaller number of writers on other subjects are members of the Union of Journalists. A rather ill-defined breakdown of Soviet authors by qualification and occupation in 1975 shows the following picture (categories appear to overlap, and figures probably refer to authors and co-authors of works issued by publishing-houses in 1975):[36]

1000 members and corresponding members of Academies of Sciences.

7000 (approx.) professors and holders of doctors' degrees.

18 000 (approx.) senior lecturers (*dotsenty*) and holders of candidates' degrees.

Over 6000 members of the Writers' Union.

Over 3000 members of the Union of Journalists.

855 members of the Artists' Union.

364 medical practitioners.

1655 teachers.

5386 engineering and technical workers.

1335 agricultural specialists.

These figures should be set against a total Writers' Union membership (at 1 January 1971) of 7174 and a Union of Journalists membership of 49 103 at the same date.[37]

Much the most significant authors' organisation in book publishing affairs, although only in a fairly well-defined field of publication, is the Writers' Union.[38] Not only does it administer some of the most important fiction publishing-houses (such as Sovetskii Pisatel', controlled by the USSR union, and Sovremennik, controlled by the RSFSR union), but its central secretariat and its organisations in the constituent republics exercise considerable influence over imaginative literature issued by other publishers. Until the middle of the 1960s, a satisfactory report (*otzyv*) from the appropriate authorities in the Writers' Union was required before a publishing-house could approve a work of fiction for publication.[39] Although this requirement has now been removed, organs of the Writers' Union still assess the combined draft plans of publishing-houses for all fictional works, before they are considered by the board of the State Committee for Publishing. The Union is also consulted by the State Committee for Publishing before the latter finalises plans for issuing writers' collected works; and, at least in the case of translations from foreign languages, the Union discusses publishers' proposals before editorial work on the manuscripts is planned. A deputy chairman of the Union's bureau, S. V. Sartakov, is a member of the board of the State Committee for Publishing; and the board has held joint meetings with the Union's secretariat to produce recommendations on important issues, such as improving the availability of literature from the Soviet minority nationalities. The Union's secretariat has on occasion taken the initiative in approaching the State Committee or its predecessors, as when it urged the former Committee for the Press to improve the publication of translated literature by publishing-houses in the republics.[40]

It appears that publishing-houses, now freed from the obligation to consult the Writers' Union, are paying somewhat less attention to its officials than the latter expect. A secretary of the Latvian Writers' Union complained in 1974 that the editorial office for children's literature at the Liesma publishing-house in Riga refused to listen to the Union's opinions;[41] while the director of the Udmurtiya publishing-house suggested in the same year that writers' organisations must reconcile themselves to greater selectivity on the part of publishers – particularly of those publishers which were being set targets for loss reduction under the new planning system.[42]

Former Soviet authors affirm that membership of the Writers' Union is frequently to an author's advantage in getting a work of fiction accepted for publication. The Union's secretariat, which has a high proportion of Party members, is believed to retain the effective power to prevent publication of a literary work, to reverse a decision not to publish, and to refer cases of important controversy to the CPSU Central Committee, with whose Departments of Culture and of Propaganda it maintains close relations.[43] The Union has also been accused of intervening over the amount of 'exposure' given to popular authors: the chief editor of the Lenizdat publishing-house alleged in 1974 that the Union discouraged publishers from expressing too strong a preference for favoured authors by re-issuing their works in the year of first publication.[44]

In matters affecting its members' remuneration and welfare, the Writers' Union receives substantial financial support nominally from the publishing industry, but in fact from fiction authors collectively. It administers the Literary Fund (Litfond) as a source of grants, loans and other benefits, in practice very largely to Union members. The income of Litfond is derived from membership fees, from property and enterprises under the fund's and the Union's control, and from a levy on all publishing-houses issuing imaginative and children's literature, literary criticism and literary history. This levy is equal to 10 per cent of all fees payable to authors and translators of material falling into these categories, and it is deducted by the publisher from all such fees before transmitting the balance to the author, irrespective of whether or not he is a member of the Union.[45] Between 1967 and 1970, the income of Litfond was 17.1 million roubles, of which about nine million roubles came from the so-called publishers' contributions (really authors' contributions).[46] For graphical publications and musical or musicological works, the deductions to the Artistic Fund and the Musical Fund are 2 per cent and 5 per cent respectively; and from all fees paid for socio-political, popular scientific and informational books, 0.5 per cent is deducted to the Journalists' Fund.

7

Printing, paper and supplies

Both at the level of the individual publishing-house and at that of national administration, Soviet publishing has a more complex involvement with the printing industry which serves it than the customer–supplier relationship which is usual in Western publishing. This chapter studies the organisation and economics of Soviet printing as they affect book publishing, and the administrative and contractual relations between printer and publisher. This is followed by an examination of the very direct significance to Soviet publishers of the supply of printers' materials, especially paper.

7.1. *Printing: administrative and economic position*

The State Committee for Publishing, Printing and the Book Trade is the government organ responsible for the printing industry. It plans and regulates the activity of printing enterprises through the same hierarchy of republic and local administrations which supervise publishing-houses. Most of the printers not subordinated directly to one of the State Committee's organs remain subject to its instructions on many operational matters. The only exceptions are printers serving scientific and technical information services (controlled by the State Committee for Science and Technology) and those administered by the Party itself, which include the enterprises printing most newspapers and some journals.

The State Committee for Publishing and its subordinate committees in the republics plan the printing industry's development and yearly performance in conjunction with Gosplan on the lines described in 4.4, working from the range and capacity of available printing establishments, newly commissioned plant, anticipated supply of paper and other materials, and the stated requirements of publishers and others ordering printed matter of all descriptions. These requirements are expressed entirely in quantitative terms (total amount in printed sheet-copies, with a breakdown by types of printing process and binding required, and a separate statement of the amounts needed for export); and volume of production is the most important of the planning indicators set for each printing enterprise by its superior organ, although the indicator of production expressed in monetary terms is now being given increased prominence, and printers' performance has recently been related also to the publishing plans of the publishers they serve.

The allocation of printing capacity to each publishing-house is made by the organs of the State Committee for Publishing. The precise distribution of work is carried out by 'associations' (*ob"edineniya*) of printing enterprises where they exist. The only discretion allowed to the printer under this system is the detailed negotiation of the contracts between himself and the publishers. In the same way, he can vary only the detail in the contracts for the supply of his most important materials, including paper, under another allocation scheme, described below. Since his superior organ must lay down, or at least give approval to, his planning indicator figures for sales, profit, profitability and wages fund, and since the prices for his work are centrally regulated, the printer's scope for decision within his enterprise is narrowed to matters of technical decision, detailed internal planning, staffing and incentive payments (within the limits of the salary fund and ruling national guidelines), and the use, again within limits, of bank credit.[1]

A revised list of printing charges was introduced in 1967 with the transfer of printers to the new planning and incentive system. It gave an average increase in charges of 5.2 per cent over the previous list,[2] and was intended to allow an average profitability in printing enterprises of 24 per cent of average production costs. Printing is, indeed, a profit-making industry in Soviet terms, and the State Committee for Publishing regards the profits made by the printing enterprises under its control as 'covering' the losses incurred by publishing in some of the union republics.[3] Much of the capital investment in the printing industry is, however, financed by payments from the state budget: between 1966 and 1970, 58 per cent of capital investment came from central funds and 42 per cent from printing enterprises' own resources. The intention, however, is to increase investment by the enterprises themselves, with some use of long-term credit, to three-quarters of the total.[4]

The quality of printing work is checked by the State Inspectorate for the Quality of Publications, a department of the State Committee for Publishing. The Inspectorate may impose penalties, such as the forfeiture of incentive payments, on printing staff found responsible for very poor work or the breach of state standards and technical instructions.[5]

As in other sectors of industry, a programme was begun in 1973 to set up 'associations' to merge printing enterprises, combining them in a few cases with research facilities and in some instances, particularly in the peripheral republics, with publishing-houses, in order to improve cooperation between printers and publishers at local level and to relieve the republics' publishing administrations of much detailed coordinating work. However, present policy appears to be that major publishing-houses in Moscow and Leningrad should not be linked in permanent associations with printing establishments, although some central publishers, such as Politizdat and Nauka, have maintained their own printing facilities for many years, and can be regarded as 'associations' in themselves. The other large publishers use the services of a wide circle of printers with different specialities and equipment, and draw on printing capacity on an all-union scale: the installed capacity of printing plant in the Belorussian SSR in 1971, for example, was estimated to be two-and-a-half to three times greater than was needed to meet the publishing demands of that republic alone.[6] What appears to be an important innovation is the intention announced in 1977 to set up an 'all-union association' entitled 'Nauchno-Tekhnicheskaya Kniga'. The few details released at the time of writing state that the new association is intended to group fourteen central scientific and technical publishers with eleven printing enterprises, although the publishers are to retain a degree of separate identity.[7]

7.2. *Printer and publisher*

The contractual relations between printer and publisher are at present (1977) regulated by the 'Temporary basic conditions for the fulfilment by printing enterprises of publishing-houses' orders for the production of books, journals and graphical publications',[8] introduced in 1971, which are a compulsory element in all contracts. They supersede the 'Basic conditions' of 1965 in providing for the 'attachment' (*prikreplenie*) of publishing-houses to printers over extended periods of time (a change intended to contribute to stable planning by both parties under the new planning and incentive system), and in increasing the penalties for non-observance, especially for failure to meet important planning and delivery dates. In 1973 the State Committee for Publishing ordered that the publishers' annual publication plans should become another datum line for assessing printers' fulfilment of their obligations.

The process of concluding contracts between publisher and printer, as laid down in the 'Temporary conditions', follows the following sequence. The publishing-house, on receiving its superior organ's approval of its annual publication plan, sends the plan, with a breakdown by quarters, to the printer or printers to which it has been 'attached' by the State Committee for Publishing. The parties then reach preliminary agreement over the timing of production for the annual and quarterly plans, which themselves become a part of the contract. The publisher must try to obtain final recommendations for edition sizes from the book trade wholesale organisations by 1 October of the year preceding the plan year, and any alterations to the plan required by the superior organ must be notified to publisher and printer by 10 October. When the printer has received approval from *his* superior organ of his planned output for the year, and has attempted to reconcile this with the plans of all the publishers which he supplies, he sends a draft contract for the year's work to each publisher, which must be agreed or objected to within ten days.

During the year, quarterly plans for composing and printing work, and 'plan-orders' (*plany-zayavki*) for each month's production, are agreed on the basis of the publishing plans. The printer is obliged to include in his monthly production plan all titles from the publishing plan which have been signed for printing by the publisher by the 27th of the previous month, up to a limit of one-third of the titles specified for that quarter, although the State Committee for Publishing may permit the limits to be breached in exceptional cases and for urgent publications. The publisher, for his part, may include in his monthly plan-orders only those works for which the supply of paper and other materials is assured, whether the responsibility for that supply lies with the publisher or with the printer, as described in 7.3.

The conditions of the contract set out a large number of monetary penalties to be levied for contraventions, most of them intended to ensure observance of schedules. For example, delay by either party in the transmission of contracts or publishing plans brings liability to a forfeit of 50r. for each day by which the limit is exceeded, up to a 500r. maximum. Any delay in the production and delivery of material relating to Party congresses, Central Committee plenums, sessions of the USSR Supreme Soviet, and of publications for important events and anniversaries, leads to a forfeit of double the normal amount; and a printer consuming more paper than that allowed by the norms for each type of publication must compensate the publishing-house (where it supplied the paper) for the excess consumption, besides forfeiting a further sum equal to the value of the excess.

The printer in any country is entirely dependent on the publishing-house for a supply of prepared manuscripts, and for a thorough specification of the design and production processes to be applied to each title and of the number of copies to be printed. In the Soviet Union, where both printer and publisher are expected to prepare and adhere to a detailed annual plan, the specifications for the bulk of an entire year's production are imparted to the printer only when he receives the publishers' approved publication plans for the coming year. The remainder is the 'reserve' of up to 20 per cent of the publisher's output, which may be used – though again on the publisher's initiative – during the course of the plan year. The approved publication plans usually arrive too late for the printer to incorporate their data into much of his own production and financial planning for the year to which they refer, and it has in any case been alleged that publication plans often contain insufficient technical detail for the printer's purposes; so the printer is frequently forced to plan with approximations based on the previous year's figures, and in some measure by intuition.[9]

A further obstacle to the efficient operation of both parties, which affects the smaller publishing-houses in particular, is the difficulty of ensuring an effective 'fit' between the character of the publisher's desired output and the available printing facilities, when the assignment of the one to the other is made from above by the State Committee for Publishing. It was reported in 1975 that the L'vov publishing-house Kamenyar had to have fiction titles in editions of over 100 000 printed on flat-bed presses because the printing enterprise allotted to it did not possess the much faster rotary presses, for which incidentally printing charges would have been lower.[10] On the other hand it has been noted that the attachment of a single major publisher to an appropriate large printing enterprise can be highly advantageous: the director of Prosveshchenie, the largest textbook publisher in the USSR, has remarked on the great improvement in quality brought about by giving his house the entire resources of the Saratov printing combine.[11]

These constraints imposed by planning practice on the coordination of publishers' and printers' work exacerbate a difference in interest between the two subsectors, to which Soviet commentators have often drawn attention, and which itself stems from the planning criteria imposed on them. The publishing-house has the greatest incentive to give first priority to the fulfilment of its annual publication plan and the overall profitability of the titles in that plan; hence it requires from its printers the maximum speed and minimum cost in the production of each title. The printer's principal interest, on the other hand, is in the efficient use of his equipment to meet the quantitative and economic indicators in his own production and financial plans. Despite the fact that one of his own planning elements is now the publisher's annual publication plan, his total output in printed sheet-copies remains one of the most important indicators laid down for him, and makes him reluctant to accept publishers' orders for small editions, which increase the amount of preparatory work that has to be done on each title at the expense of his total output figures. This resistance to small editions among printers may well have been a factor, in addition to the obvious one of cost, in the decisions taken in the Ukrainian SSR and elsewhere in the early 1970s to produce small-edition publications (of, say, 1000 copies or less) by reproduction from typewriting wherever possible.[12]

Notwithstanding these differences of interest, the interdependence of printer and publisher is such that neither will readily venture a stand on the letter of a contract or regulation, even when the other party's action lays it open to a well-founded claim. The delays in plan fulfilment which a claimant would suffer, and the likelihood of spoiling future relations with an enterprise to which the claimant might remain 'attached' for years by the State Committee for Publishing, have – it is alleged – made a resort to arbitration a rare event, and 'mutual amnesties' over penalties are common.[13]

7.3. Paper and other supplies

The nature and operation of the organs supplying the publishing and printing industries have been outlined in 4.4. The Chief Administration for Material and Technical Supply (Glavsnabsbyt) of the State Committee for Publishing plans the supply of paper, binding materials, inks, type metal, etc., and submits indents to Gosplan and

Gossnab for the sector as a whole.[14] Glavsnabsbyt operates on *khozraschet*, depending on an addition to the wholesale price of the goods handled to meet its overheads and provide a profit: for example, 13.50r. per ton of paper, 17r. per 1000 metres of binding materials, and 3 per cent of the price of other goods.[15] In 1974, Glavsnabsbyt's supply offices in Moscow and Leningrad were the first such organs in any industry to be transferred to the new planning and financial system. This makes the payment of full incentives dependent not only on meeting the year's total turnover plan, but also on the complete execution of delivery contracts.[16]

Glavsnabsbyt's global orders for materials are founded on the orders submitted to it by printers and publishers, using (in 1972) eighty types of form for some 3000 items of supply.[17] These orders must be sent in by the enterprises in May or June of the year preceding the plan year, at an early stage in the finalisation of their annual production and publication plans, with no assurance that the total output of the goods ordered will enable their requirements to be met in full. The consequent tendency to over-order is well recognised, and is common to the rest of Soviet industry for the same reasons.

The State Committee for Publishing has the duty of establishing the demand for printing paper and putting its requirements to the paper industry; but Soviet publishers have often made it clear that the most immediate limitation on the number of titles they issue and, even more, on the number of copies printed, is the shortage of paper. However carefully their publication plans are prepared, they must be modified if necessary to fit the paper quota allotted to the publishing-house, which is usually notified after the publication plan has been drawn up.[18] Decisions to reissue depend even more crucially on paper supply than do decisions on new titles to be published, since a publishing-house and its superior organ will be reluctant to allow fewer titles to appear in the annual publication plan than in that of the previous year, even if this requires a reduction in edition sizes. The chief editor of the Meditsina house claimed in 1972 that the volume of orders received for his house's books would justify ten times the number of copies of reissued titles that their paper quota allowed.[19]

The figures available to indicate the effect on book publishing of inadequate paper supplies allow only a very incomplete picture, but there is no question that the shortfall from demand is very considerable, and the shortfall even from planned output and variety is substantial. Between 1965 and 1970, the average annual growth in the production of suitable paper was only 0.6 per cent more than the growth in the population of the USSR.[20] Over the first four years of the ninth Five-Year Plan (1971–4) printers were supplied with 50 000 metric tons of paper less than the amount planned.[21] It was stated in 1975 that only thirty-four of the sixty-five types of printing paper provided for by official standards were actually being produced, and that the proportion of No. 1 (higher-quality) paper was not increasing but remaining at 22–24 per cent of output.[22] The causes of under-supply have been variously attributed, but while some of them are certainly to be found in the shortcomings of the paper industry (slow construction of new plant, heavy losses through poor storage and transport, and production planned in tons rather than in square metres), it is equally certain that the volume of book production has suffered since the mid-1960s from the decision to devote such increase as there was in paper supplies to enlarging the circulation of journals.[23] The extremely large volume of paper consumed in the production of forms and other official stationery has also been claimed to affect adversely supplies for book publishing: in the RSFSR alone, 90 000 tons of paper per year were being used for these documents in 1975 – the equivalent of half the paper used for the republic's entire book production.[24] The assurance reported from the paper industry in 1971, that paper supplies would be adequate for publishing in 1980 and would cease to be the 'keystone' of the planning structure,[25] has so far shown little sign of being borne out. The tenth Five-Year Plan envisages an increase in paper and card production of only 15–25 per cent between 1976 and 1980, and growth in supplies to publishing is expected to be no more than 10 per cent over the same period.[26]

Until the mid-1960s, paper was allocated physically to publishing-houses, was paid for by them and transmitted to the printers from their own stores as required. The inefficiency of this system led the (then) Committee for the Press to introduce a centralised warehousing system in 1965–7 for those publishers under its direct control, operated by Glavsnabsbyt. Publishers were notified by Glavsnabsbyt of the amounts of paper allocated to them; but, since the paper continued to be paid for directly by the publishers, printers had little incentive to economise in its use, except for the penalties incurred by exceeding consumption norms. In 1969, therefore, responsibility for purchasing paper was finally transferred to the printers serving central publishing-houses, and in 1974 it was announced that this responsibility was to be extended to include binding materials.

Under the new purchasing system for paper, the printer may not charge the publishing-house for any paper which he has used beyond the norms set for consumption in the type of work concerned.[27] The sequence of events in obtaining paper under the new system is as follows: within fifteen days of the State Committee for Publishing confirming a publishing-house's planned output for the year in printed sheet-copies, Glavsnabsbyt notifies the publisher of his allocation of paper and binding materials for the year. Within the next five days, the publisher must inform Glavsnabsbyt how the paper should be distributed between the printers to which the publishing-house has been attached. The publisher also sends the printers a specification of the amount and varieties of paper which will reach them from his allocation. Glavsnabsbyt in due course notifies each printer of the total amount of paper which may be delivered to him in each quarter, and a contract is signed between each printer and Glavsnabsbyt for delivery and payment.

The difficulties caused to both publisher and printer by delays in the allocation of paper are readily understandable, and apparently widespread. In the case of the Prosveshchenie publishing-house, which has to work to especially strict deadlines in issuing some 200 million copies of school textbooks by 1 July each year, their director stated in 1972 that they ideally required notification of printing capacity allocations three months before the beginning of each plan year, and of paper allocations two months before. In fact, the allocations for 1972 were sent to them in February of that same year, until which time relations with their thirty-odd printers had to be maintained by gentlemen's agreements (*na chestnom slove*).[28]

Measures to foster an economic use of paper have been introduced at different points in the publication process, particularly in the last ten years. The power of the State Committee for Publishing to set norms for paper consumption, and to allocate paper to publishing-houses and other organisations, has already been described. An order of 1969 cited examples of books making wasteful use of paper, and asked publishers to reduce the average size of books by at least 5 per cent by increasing the number of words per page.[29] In 1972 publishers' editorial staff were given an incentive to reduce the length of manuscripts being prepared for publication, by the use of a formula which allowed, for instance, an original manuscript of nine sheets, shortened to eight-and-a-half sheets, to be credited as nine-and-a-quarter sheets by the editor towards his work quota.[30] Even more recently, in 1975, the board of the State Committee for Publishing decided on the more drastic step of placing maximum limits on the length of most types of non-fictional book: twenty printer's sheets for scholarly publications; ten sheets for popular scientific literature and for collections of articles issued by institutions; and four sheets for mass political literature. Permission must now be given by the State Committee for Publishing for the issue of any work exceeding these limits.[31] A competition for publishing-houses was inaugurated in 1976, carrying a first prize of 1000r. for the collective making the best suggestion for saving paper.

Finally, in an attempt to encourage the re-use of paper and simultaneously satisfy more of the demand for light fiction, a scheme was launched in 1974 under which, in exchange for at least twenty kilogrammes of waste paper, individuals were given coupons allowing them to buy a copy of such works as Il'f and Petrov's *The twelve chairs*, other Russian and Soviet novels, Andersen's fairy tales, and *The hound of the Baskervilles*, printed in special editions of up to 500 000. Further titles have been printed under the scheme in subsequent years, and it has remained extremely popular despite some organisational confusion and cases of speculation and forgery of the coupons.[32]

8

The book trade

The term 'book trade' is applied here to the wholesale and retail trading organisations which distribute books from the publisher to their point of sale. The relationship between publishers and the book trade in the Soviet Union is an even more intimate one than that which exists in the West. Not only is the Soviet book trade the only channel through which the publisher can make his sales, and an important means of communicating public reaction to each title, but it is a subsector, along with publishing, of one centrally planned and administered industrial and distributive operation. This chapter considers the structure and economic position of the Soviet book trade; the transactions between publishing-houses and book trade organisations in matters of planning, contracts and the transmission of orders; and the features of certain types of trade outlet (the consumer cooperative network, the second-hand trade and the export trade) to which publishing policy has given special attention.

8.1. *The structure of the book trade*

Throughout the Soviet period, trade in books has never been under the jurisdiction of the state's general trade administration (the present Ministry of Trade and its predecessors), but has always been the responsibility of cultural, educational or more specialised state organs. The State Committee for Publishing, Printing and the Book Trade plans and supervises the book trade through the same hierarchy as that which administers publishing and printing. Its powers over the distribution of printed matter (in contrast with its powers over printing and publishing) are, however, confined to non-periodical publications. In respect of these, it is responsible for the overall planning and development of all book trade networks, and for the direct administration of the 'state' network immediately subordinated to the State Committee itself. Distribution of newspapers and journals is largely carried out by the separate network of Soyuzpechat', which is administered by the USSR Ministry of Communications, even though publishers issuing periodical titles are mostly controlled by the State Committee for Publishing in the same way as book publishing-houses – which, indeed, many of them also are. Soyuzpechat' also handles a small non-periodical trade.

The supervision of the (non-periodical) book trade by the State Committee for Publishing is exercised through its Chief Administration for the Book Trade and Book Propaganda (Glavkniga). Glavkniga manages the State Committee's own bookselling network and coordinates the operations of the other trading networks, partly through the agency of the all-union wholesaling organisation Soyuzkniga. Its other responsibilities include organisation of book imports and exports; securing better estimation of demand and edition sizes; improving the supply of books to libraries through library supply agencies; and propagating more efficient trading methods.

In the USSR, as in many other countries, the book trade organisations are for the most part not controlled by publishing enterprises, and handle books issued by many different publishers, although a few Soviet publishing-houses do administer their own, relatively small, networks. In 1974, out of a total book trade turnover of 800.8 million roubles, the 'state' book trade network directly managed by Glavkniga accounted for 65.6 per cent, the consumer cooperative network for 21.6 per cent, Soyuzpechat' for 7.8 per cent, and other networks for 4.9 per cent.[1] The smaller networks include trade outlets controlled by the Ministry of Defence, the Literary Fund, the Academy of Sciences of the USSR (chiefly the products of their publishing-house Nauka), the publishing-house Transport, and the All-Union Theatre Society.

The Soyuzkniga wholesale organisation is used by Glavkniga, which directly controls it, to coordinate the delivery of books from the central publishing-houses to all the trade networks. It circulates publishers' plans to the trading organisations, informs them through a regular bulletin of publications not included in the annual plans, estimates the demand for each title from pre-publication orders collected by the networks, analyses demand for different types of literature from surveys of its own, and makes proposals for edition sizes to publishers. It compiles delivery plans for each central publisher, concludes contracts with publishers for the supply of titles to the state book trade network, and manages the Central Wholesale Book Warehouse.[2] It coordinates, and passes to publishers, proposals for reissuing titles found by the trade to be in heavy demand, and organises redistribution of stocks by means of the bulletin *Spros i predlozhenie* and through wholesale book fairs.

Central publishing-houses, except those with their own retail outlets, may normally deliver books for distribution to Soyuzkniga alone, and local publishing-houses only to their own republic- or *oblast'*-level book trade organisation. Delivery to other organisations is allowed only with the permission of the State Committee for Publishing or of Soyuzkniga. (In a case in 1972, the publishing-house Planeta sold the complete edition of a book to the Berezka foreign-currency trading organisation, and was fined 10 000r.)[3] Soyuzkniga, in its turn, concludes contracts with local book trade organisations in the state network (*knigotorgi*), and with other bookselling networks, for the supply of central publishers' titles.

8.2. *The economic position of the book trade*

Glavkniga and Soyuzkniga both operate on *khozraschet*, the basis of which in Glavkniga's case is simply the performance of the trading organs subordinated to it, while Soyuzkniga covers its costs by a deduction from the discount given by publishers to the book trade. Trading organisations at republic level are also normally on *khozraschet*, but many of the smaller units in the book trade (bookshops, library supply agencies, and some wholesale warehouses) work on 'partial *khozraschet*', which indicates a measure of cross-subsidisation.[4]

Transfer of the bookselling organisations to the new planning and incentive system began on a large scale in 1971, after earlier experimental transfers, and was intended to be complete in 1975. Under the new system, the two most significant indicators set for each enterprise are sales and profits, which have to be confirmed at the planning stage by its superior organ. Other indicators, such as labour, wages and overheads, are nominally determined by the enterprise itself, but it is obliged to have regard to the targets set by its superior organ for payments to the state budget, capital investment, limits on the deductions to incentive funds, and deductions to support the higher administration of the trade.[5]

Since incentive funds are formed primarily from profits, the chief source of which is the discount received from publishers (either directly or through the wholesaler), the most obvious stimulus of incentives is towards increased turnover. This tendency was already noted and regretted in the 1960s by some figures in the book trade, who saw it leading to the treatment of books as simply 'merchandise' and to large orders for books in heavy demand.[6] Bookshops are made even more reluctant to order slow-selling titles by the standard turnover periods for their stock set by higher authority: complaints have been made that these periods are often 150–180 days, while some books (especially textbooks and reference works) may be intended to sell over a period of five or six years before being reprinted or superseded.[7]

A 'conventional' example of the generation of incentive funds suggests that the formulae for their payment out of profits are intended to give equal emphasis to growth in profits and in sales. Superior organs are allowed to alter the amount of the payments within certain limits; they may, for example, reduce payments (and hence the size of the incentive fund) by 10 or 20 per cent in an enterprise showing poor performance. The enterprise itself may refuse or reduce incentive payments to staff responsible for 'unjustified' orders to publishers, or other failings.[8]

The standard rate of discount given by publishers, both central and local, to wholesale organisations in the Glavkniga network, is 25 per cent: that is, the price charged by the publisher in this transaction is 25 per cent below the retail price (*nominal*), which has been calculated by the publisher according to the size and type of book (see 2.2). The discount is reduced to 15 per cent for sets of the works of Marx, Engels and Lenin, and for the *Bol'shaya sovetskaya entsiklopediya* (*Great Soviet encyclopedia*).[9] Deliveries from the wholesale organisation are made to other enterprises at widely varying discounts on the retail price, fixed with the aim of ensuring that the wholesaler's costs are covered and at the same time that trading organisations in remoter areas have the opportunity to show a profit. The discounts allowed by Soyuzkniga, for instance, range from 12 per cent (for the Moscow and Leningrad bookselling organs) to 60–70 per cent for the organs in Magadan and Yakutsk.[10]

In practice, most book trade organs appear to secure a low profit margin. Soyuzkniga's Central Wholesale Book Warehouse reported a profit of only 1 per cent of turnover in 1970. The Warehouse claimed that the low discount of 15 per cent on the *Bol'shaya sovetskaya entsiklopediya* would have reduced their 1971 profits by over 140 000r. because of the over-plan production of one volume, had not the Committee for the Press 'assisted' them.[11] Nevertheless, the profits of Glavkniga's book trade system rose from 8.6 million roubles in 1967 to about 40 million roubles in 1975,[12] compared with a much slower rise in the value of sales over the same period (from 302.6 million to 536.2 million roubles).[13]

A good deal of criticism has been levelled at the present discount policy, which has been little modified since its introduction in 1940. It is pointed out that even the highest discounts allowed may be quite unrealistic: for example, while the average retail value of one standard parcel of books was 13.18r. in 1972, the cost of posting it to Yakutsk, even by surface mail, was 12.53r.[14] The low profit levels of many publishers have been used to justify making no increase in the average discount, but there has been support for a more differentiated structure, to stimulate the sales of slow-selling categories of book and to improve the economic position of the book trade in rural areas, which is largely in the hands of the consumer cooperatives. Discounts allowed to consumer cooperatives are usually somewhat lower than those given to enterprises in the Glavkniga network. Calculations published in 1974 showed an average level of 22.5 per cent, which is regarded as insufficient for the consumer cooperative book trade to operate on *khozraschet*, for which it was estimated that an average discount of 29 per cent would be needed.[15] This low profitability has led some smaller cooperative book trade organisations to increase profits by disproportionate sales of stationery and other cultural and recreational goods, which in a few cases, in 1969, accounted for over three-quarters of their turnover.[16] Even in the Glavkniga trading network, about one-third of total retail turnover in recent years has been from goods other than books.[17]

Expenditure on publicity measures by book trade organs is very low by Western standards, since demand for most types of work is so much in excess of supply that it needs little stimulus. The Leningrad book trade organisation Lenkniga, which claims to spend more on publicity than most, spent only 51 000r. (0.44 per cent of turnover, or 4.22 per cent of distribution costs) for this purpose in 1974.[18]

8.3. *The book trade and the publishing-house*

Relations between the publishing-houses and the book trade centre on three principal types of transaction: firstly, the collection by the book trade of orders for titles announced by publishers and the ensuing recommendations made by the trade for edition sizes; secondly, the delivery of the books by the publisher to the wholesale trading organisations; and finally, the financial responsibility of both parties for unsold stock.

Book trade organs are said to be only rarely consulted by publishers in the compilation of their publishing plans,[19] although some houses circulate their editorial preparation plans to the trade, and official instructions emphasise the importance of such consultation, particularly between republic or *oblast'* trading organisations and their local publishing-houses. The book trade's first acquaintance with new publications is therefore usually made with the delivery of copies of publishers' annual publication plans. Central publishers' annual plans are to be distributed to the book trade, under the recently revised timetable, by 1 January of the year before that to which they refer, as described in 4.6, although they do in fact arrive as late as August. The wholesale organisation contracting for deliveries then has seventy-five days in which to establish demand before informing each publisher how many copies of each title it wishes to order. The problems created by the necessity to prepare such orders for some 50 000 titles, from publication plans arriving over a period of a few months at most have been remarked upon. The equivalent time limits allowed by publishers in the union republics are even shorter: in the Ukrainian SSR, individual bookshops and library supply agencies are allowed fifty days from the receipt of the plan, and *oblast'* wholesale organisations sixty days, in which to submit orders to the republic wholesalers.[20]

The processes by which book trade organisations determine the number of copies to be ordered of each title vary with the type of literature concerned. For social and political literature, consultation with the local Party organs before orders are placed is regarded as important. Many categories of literature cannot be ordered in advance of publication because demand is known to be far greater than supply, and popular books from central publishing-houses are not usually obtainable through the book trade's postal order system Kniga-pochtoi.[21] In the Estonian SSR, pre-publication orders are accepted only for 'specialist' publications, but even so, one bookshop alone in Tallinn was unable to fill 40 000 such orders in 1972.[22] In the RSFSR, pre-publication orders in 1973 were responsible for only about a quarter of the number of copies actually ordered by the book trade from publishers, with the remainder being added from an intuitive estimate of likely sales.[23] It is accepted that, in any case, smaller shops are unlikely to estimate demand accurately, and orders for the smaller outlets are often estimated and placed by trading organs at a higher level.

The work of the *tirazhnye komissii* in resolving disagreements over edition sizes between publishers and the book trade has been described in 5.8. The wholesale organisation contracting to buy from a publisher must be given the opportunity to see the proofs of a book, or a copy of the manuscript, before it is signed for printing. It then has the right to amend the number of copies ordered, within two days of receiving the proofs, by a maximum of 15 per cent in either direction, unless the amount of the author's fee would thereby be increased.[24] Publishers find this provision irksome – understandably – but paper limitations will in any case very often force them to print fewer copies than the number ordered. It has been estimated that, overall, orders placed with publishers by the book trade amount to one-and-a-half times or twice the number of copies eventually issued.[25] For works issued in large edition sizes the consequences can be very drastic: the publishing-house Mir had to take the decision to print only 220 000 copies of Joy Adamson's *Pippa's challenge* (*Pippa brosaet vyzov*, 1974), after receiving 500 000 orders.[26] In such cases, Soyuzkniga and other wholesalers buying from the publisher will fill orders received from their trading networks on a proportional basis – though the 'proportion' used is not the proportion of one trading organisation's orders to the total number of orders for a given work, but the proportion of that organisation's planned turnover to the trade's total planned turnover.[27] The rate of sales in the book retail outlets is increasing as demand continues to rise further above supply. Between 1971 and 1973, book trade stocks increased by 9.2 per cent, while retail turnover rose by 25.6 per cent; and between 1971 and 1974 deliveries to the book trade from central publishers grew at less than half the rate of increase in orders (20.9 per cent as against 53.1 per cent).[28]

Orders from trading organisations which appear unjustifiably low may be amended by Glavkniga in agreement with the appropriate republic's book trade organ, in which case the organisation concerned must within three days reconsider the quantity it requires or give reasons for confirming its original figure. Works considered especially important or urgent may be distributed from publishers to the book trade on the authority of Glavkniga, or its equivalents in the republics, without requesting orders, and must be paid for by the recipient trading organisations. The same authorities may reduce the size of orders for any title at their discretion, without the agreement of the organisations placing the orders, before the delivery contracts with the publishers are signed.[29]

The year's contract signed between the publishing-house and

Soyuzkniga (or any other wholesaler) is followed by agreement between the parties on quarterly delivery plans, specifying titles, retail prices and number of copies. However, since the publishing-house may modify its own quarterly publication plans in the light of, for example, printing delays or paper shortages, the terms of quarterly delivery plans, and even annual contracts, with the book trade have been described as having a 'formal' character.[30] The publishing-house is not debarred from attempting to sell more copies than the number provided for in the contract. Since 1966, the book trade has been allowed to accept from publishers additional copies of books, beyond the contracted amount, to be sold on a sale-or-return basis (*na komissionnykh nachalakh*).[31] The publishing-house must obtain from its superior organ agreement on the number of copies to be distributed on this basis, and the trading organisation accepting them will normally hold them for two years before returning unsold copies, and sometimes for a third year at a reduced price. The usual discount of 25 per cent is given to the wholesaler, while the publisher must bear the cost of unsold copies, and any loss caused by price reductions. Although publishers are free to conclude such sale-or-return agreements with the book trade for any title, it is still an exceptional practice, and is likely to remain so whilst publishers are prevented by other imposed priorities from responding in full to major elements of reader demand.

Financial liability for unsold copies bought from publishers by the book trade under annual contracts has since 1964 been divided equally between the parties, where lack of sales has been judged to be due to the book's 'loss of significance'.[32] Lists of titles to be written off, making use of reports from retail outlets, must be submitted by Soyuzkniga and other wholesalers to the State Committees for Publishing at union and republic level, stating which books should have their losses shared in this way. (A fund to cover those losses borne by the book trade is formed by a deduction of 2 per cent from retail turnover.)[33] The ninth annual list of books to be written off, in 1974, contained some 4000 titles, with an estimated one million copies to be pulped in Moscow alone.[34]

Despite this and other absolute figures sometimes quoted to show the quantity of books remaining unsold for many years (for example, books worth one-third of a million roubles warehoused at Yaroslavl' in 1974),[35] the proportion of copies subject to price reduction and writing-off is much smaller than is common in the Western book trade, though it varies considerably with the subject-matter of the books. At 1 September 1972, figures from the book trade's annual stocktaking showed that, of copies published in 1970, 1969 and 1968, only 1.92 per cent, 1.13 per cent and about 1 per cent respectively remained unsold.[36] Only about 2 per cent of retail sales in 1975 were accounted for by books disposed of at reduced prices.[37] The products of some provincial publishers, however, appear to be much more difficult to sell than the average figures suggest. The 1975 stocktaking showed that, of copies issued by the Perm *oblast'* publishing-house between 1971 and 1973, 25.9 per cent were still in trade stocks, and 38.8 per cent of those from the publishing-house of Kaliningrad *oblast'*.[38]

8.4. *The consumer cooperative book trade network*

Book distribution in the rural areas of the USSR is undertaken by the trading network of the consumer cooperatives, except in the Baltic republics and the Moldavian SSR, where the rural, as well as the urban book trade is controlled directly by the republics' state committees for publishing. The distinction between the two systems is chiefly an administrative one, since the cooperative associations function in practice as the rural branch of the state retail network.

The quality of book supply outside the towns has been the subject of criticism for many years, prompting Central Committee decrees in 1960, 1964 and 1967, the last of which led to the creation of specialised book trading organs within the cooperative trade network at republic and *oblast'* level, supplied primarily by an all-union wholesale office, Tsentrokoopkniga, which is administered by the Central Union of Consumer Societies (Tsentrosoyuz). The cooperative trading network suffers, like the state network, from the problem of under-supply by publishers. Orders by cooperatives from central publishers' plans for 1972 totalled 150 million roubles, compared with an eventual delivery plan of 69.8 million roubles.[39] This shortfall is claimed to be aggravated for the rural book trade by Soyuzkniga's practice, where a title is published in fewer copies than the number ordered, of sending even those books intended specifically for rural workers to both rural and urban bookshops in the same proportion.[40] Multi-volume works ordered on subscription are stated to be in particularly short supply for the cooperative book trade. Of the 520 000 sets being printed of the *Detskaya entsiklopediya* (*Children's encyclopedia*, published by Pedagogika from

1971 and to be in twelve volumes), the cooperative trade is receiving only 43 000, although it serves nearly half the USSR's population.[41]

8.5. *The second-hand book trade*

Trade in second-hand books has been strongly encouraged in the last decade by the State Committee for Publishing and its predecessors, as a means of mitigating shortages of new books, especially fiction, children's literature and textbooks. Besides increasing the supply of books to the personal buyer, second-hand purchases have been organised by Soyuzkniga to improve the holdings of rural libraries. The number of shops and departments buying and selling second-hand publications has increased dramatically, from just over 200 in 1965 to over 2000 in 1973.[42] In 1974 about 28 million roubles was paid by Soviet bookshops for second-hand material.[43] The aim of the State Committee for Publishing is to increase second-hand sales to 10 per cent of total book trade turnover.

The Soviet press has reported that second-hand bookshops are suffering competition from illegal 'speculation' by private individuals who, because of the book shortage, are able to offer (and demand) much higher prices than the official second-hand trade. Figures of up to 25r. for a copy of *The three musketeers* have been quoted.[44]

8.6. *Book exports*

High importance is accorded to the export of Soviet books, for both political and commercial reasons. Between 1970 and 1975, annual output of Soviet books in non-Soviet languages showed a doubling in the number of titles and a tripling in the number of copies issued annually.[45] This importance is reflected in the various kinds of priority and special incentives granted for the preparation and handling of books to be sent abroad. In planning their paper and printing requirements, publishers are instructed to state separately the amounts needed for export orders. Orders from abroad for books intended for a foreign readership are not normally cut back because of paper shortages.[46] Where an edition is to be delivered by a printer in more than one instalment, copies for export must be sent in the first instalment. Further, the State Committee for Publishing administers a special incentive fund into which is paid 0.6 per cent of the wholesale rouble price of books delivered abroad, plus 10 per cent of the receipts in foreign currency from sales. The fund is distributed among publishers, printers and Soyuzkniga departments to reward high-quality work and speedy delivery.[47]

In 1977, in an important administrative innovation, a new department was set up within the State Committee for Publishing to bring together the work of producing and distributing Soviet publications intended for a non-Soviet readership. The new Chief Administration for the Publication and Export Delivery of Soviet Literature for the Foreign Reader is to have the export-orientated publishing-houses Progress, Mir, Russkii Yazyk, Avrora and Vneshtorgizdat directly subordinated to it. It will also coordinate the planning and production of all literature intended for foreign readers issued by other publishers. It will handle orders for such publications received from the all-union foreign trading organisation Mezhdunarodnaya Kniga, which is responsible for all export and import transactions for books, periodicals, slides and sound recordings to and from the USSR; and it will cooperate with Mezhdunarodnaya Kniga in studying the markets for Soviet publications abroad.[48]

Exports of printed matter from the USSR were valued at over 23.4 million roubles in 1973, rising to over 29.3 million roubles in 1974.[49] Over half the books exported were in Russian or other languages of the USSR, and over half again were exported to socialist countries, with France the largest buyer among capitalist countries.[50]

9

Special kinds of publication

In its application of instructions, priorities and incentives, Soviet book publishing policy distinguishes between many different kinds of book, categorised in a variety of ways. For some purposes, distinctions are drawn between works in different subjects, for other purposes they are drawn between works intended for different groups of reader, or recognition is given to the special conditions under which certain kinds of work are produced. The two main reasons for discrimination in treatment are to produce more of certain types of work (sometimes by producing fewer of others), and to produce works which are, by a variety of criteria, 'better'. This chapter deals with important types of book identified in the administration of Soviet publishing, and describes the distinctive treatments accorded to each. Two major groups of book aimed at a general readership are considered: fiction, and 'mass' political and social literature. Books for more specific user groups are treated under the headings: textbooks; specialised scholarly works, in particular those in science and technology; and children's books. Finally, the following types of material are treated, which are prepared and published under special conditions: works published for libraries; works translated from foreign languages; and works published by, or on behalf of, organisations other than publishing-houses. The chapter ends with a short account of Soviet work in forecasting demand and output for different types of publication.

9.1 Types of exceptional treatment

Publications may be singled out for exceptional treatment at any stage in their planning or production. In longer-term planning, certain types of work may be emphasised in general terms in directives for the national five-year plan, as when the directives of the 24th Party Congress for the ninth Five-Year Plan specified that particular attention should be given to improving the supply of textbooks, children's books, and some types of scientific and technical literature. More recently, the State Committee for Publishing has begun to exert more specific pressure on publishers in planning the proportion of different types of publication within the total output allowed by paper stocks. In the tenth Five-Year Plan, the State Committee intends that paper should be redistributed where necessary in order to increase production of fiction and children's books (by a total of 1000 million printed sheet-copies), medical literature (by 250–300 million) and works in non-Soviet languages (by 50 million);[1] and eight central publishing-houses normally handling scientific, technical and socio-political literature have been ordered to include the former four types of publication in their plans. In the case of fiction, an increase in production of 9.9 million copies was achieved by central publishers in 1976, explicitly at the expense of other types of work: output of socio-political, scientific and technical literature fell by 5 per cent in the same year, and was planned to fall by a further 5 per cent during the years 1977–8.[2] It appears that priorities are now felt to have been sufficiently re-weighted. The sixth Writers' Union congress in 1976 was told by a deputy chairman of the State Committee for Publishing that over 70 per cent of the paper used for the publication of books was being consumed by fiction, children's literature and textbooks, and that the State Committee believed that the balance of 30 per cent devoted to other kinds of work ought not to be allowed to fall further.[3]

Highly developed systems of differentiation between types of publication are also found in the scales for authors' fees (appendix 1) and in the tables for calculating book retail prices (appendix 2). Although both have as a basis the subject and readership of the work concerned, a comparison will show the contrast between the scope allowed to the publisher in determining an author's fee between the maximum and minimum scale points, and the far more prescriptive retail price-list, which allows very little variation by the publisher. This contrast arises from the fact that an element of incentive in fee scales (that is, in the relationship between publisher and author) is regarded as permissible in order to stimulate the submission of high-quality work, and some discretion must be allowed to the publisher to achieve this. On the other hand, in the relationship between publisher and reader, the exercise of economic discretion by an individual publisher is felt to be undesirable, and the Party and state authorities have accordingly not conceded control of book pricing policy to publishing-houses.

At the level of the individual publishing-house, the operating conditions laid down for the publisher give special recognition to

the handling of certain kinds of work. In the norms for editorial
work which are used to calculate houses' staff establishments, *all*
works falling into certain categories (including Marxist–Leninist
classics, textbooks, encyclopedias and dictionaries) are allocated to
the 'most complex' group of publications in determining the size of
the technical editing staff. In proofreading, the precautionary checking of corrected page-proofs (*chitka chistykh listov*) – in addition to
the reading of galley-proofs and first page-proofs – must be carried
out for all political literature, collected editions of an author, and
reference works, as well as for complex scientific publications, and
highly illustrated and superior-quality books. Marxist–Leninist
classics and the pronouncements of Party and government leaders
must be checked yet again at every 50 000 copies printed.[4]

9.2. *Fiction*

'Fiction' is used here to render the Russian *khudozhestvennaya
literatura*, a term which covers poetry and drama as well as
imaginative prose writing. As in most countries, works of fiction are
the most widely read category of book in the Soviet Union.[5] They
have the further distinction there of being published in numbers
which satisfy reader demand to a smaller extent than that for any
other major type of publication. The percentage of fiction (including
children's fiction) in the total number of book copies published in
the USSR rose from 10–12 in the period 1928–40, to 30–33 between
1956 and 1970, and to 38.9 in 1975.[6] Yet it was calculated that
orders for works of fiction were being met by the book trade (in the
RSFSR in 1975) to the extent of only 16.8 per cent.[7] The proportion
of fiction within total book production was regarded as unsatis-
torily low by the board of the State Committee for Publishing in its
comments on the overall 1974 plan for fiction publishing, particularly with reference to Russian and foreign classics (there were
only 114 titles by pre-Revolutionary Russian authors among the
4142 titles in the plan), and to translations of the best Soviet works
into the minority languages of the USSR. The State Committee's
departments were instructed to submit proposals for increasing the
proportion of fiction.[8] These instructions were issued before the
launching of the 'books for scrap paper' scheme described in 7.3,
and may have partly inspired this measure. An increasing willingness to expand the supply of fiction is indicated by the decision,
referred to in 9.1 above, to order a further proportional increase.

During the period 1975–80, the State Committee for Publishing intends to devote the entire planned increase in its paper supplies to raising the output of fiction, and to issue on newsprint a small number of popular works in very large editions, totalling as many as forty million copies in 1978.[9]

It was stated in 1972 that over half of the publishing-houses in the USSR were issuing at least some fiction because many local houses obtained an important part of their profit from reissues of classic writers. A consequence was that the market was becoming glutted with the works of some standard authors.[10] Unwanted duplication of modern works is also occurring: the State Committee's coordination procedures in 1976 revealed 253 works by 109 contemporary Soviet authors planned for publication by two or more publishers. Eighty-seven of the proposed editions were removed from plans in agreement with the Writers' Union.[11]

9.3. *Political and social literature*

Works on political and social topics, particularly those intended to be widely read by the Soviet public, have received a great deal of special attention from policy-makers in publishing. A Central Committee decree of 1967 was intended to remedy what was seen as a fall in the quality and an inflation in the size of such works. It approved a draft decree by the RSFSR Council of Ministers which first introduced payment to authors according to edition size for this type of material, allowed very high fees for the best political pamphlets, and reduced payment for over-long works. At the same time, Party committees were ordered to improve their supervision of publishing-houses issuing social and political literature, 'strengthening' them where necessary with suitable extra staff.[12]

Works in this category are the most direct reflection, in terms of publication, of officially inspired campaigns to instruct, exhort and celebrate. Publishing-houses are informed in advance of anniversaries and campaigns which should be given prominence in their publishing plans; but, although some works are issued on the explicit instructions of a superior organ, houses retain sufficient discretion in their choice of manuscripts to warrant frequent and critical reviews by Party and state authorities of the quality of their production for particular occasions. Among the 500-odd 'fundamental' books and pamphlets issued to Soviet readers for the fiftieth anniversary of the USSR's foundation, some Georgian and Armenian publications were said subsequently to have been much criticised for nationalist sentiments and for distortions of historical phenomena and personalities.[13] Although 'overall' annual plans are prepared by the union and republic publishing administrations for social and political literature in general, and separate plans for special campaigns, they share the characteristics of other 'overall' plans in being essentially compilations from all the contributing houses' proposed titles. The appropriate State Committee for Publishing confines itself to reducing any duplication of treatment and, on occasion, pressing a publisher to strengthen its representation of a particular topic.

Books produced to support nationwide campaigns may – statistically at least – have a substantial impact on the publishing pattern. The efforts to improve workers' economic education, for example, were accompanied by about 100 titles in 1972 and some 150 in 1973. totalling fifteen million copies. The campaign to heighten the public's awareness of the legal system resulted in 585 books and pamphlets between 1971 and 1973, including 200 'mass' pamphlets. In the approach to the thirtieth anniversary of victory in the 1941–5 war, about 600 titles on the war were planned for the period 1973–5, representing a high point in the fostering of public interest in the war which had given rise, since it took place, to about 600 million copies of works dealing with some aspect of the conflict. (It was reported in 1973 that two-thirds of mass libraries' stocks in Soviet history were made up of books on the Great Patriotic War.)[14]

The publishing administrations (in conjunction with, and probably often at the instigation of, Party organs) also review the quality of broader sectors of social and political literature at irregular intervals. The board of the State Committee for Publishing in 1973 criticised the character of recent works on atheism, finding very little aimed at the conversion of religious believers, and some faiths not dealt with at all. The chief editorial offices were ordered to bring forward proposals for instructional material on atheism, and – in consultation with the Writers' Union – for increasing the issue of fiction with an atheist message. In 1974, to improve the provision of works on scientific communism, the State Committee ordered the preparation of a long-term plan (apparently founded, again, on publishers' intentions) for books to be issued on the subject. At the same time it called for a re-definition of the specialisations of publishers handling works in the field, ordered the publisher Sovetskaya

Entsiklopediya to study the possibility of producing an encyclopedia of scientific communism, and recommended the Znanie publishing-house to begin an annual competition for the best popular work on the subject.

Accounts suggest that publishing-houses specialising in political material give particular importance to wide consultation, both with the authorities interested and inside the house itself, in considering themes to be dealt with and authors to be selected. Commissioned manuscripts reaching Politizdat are read simultaneously by two senior editorial staff, 'to bring out any divergent views at an early stage', and are usually also sent to one or more authoritative external referees. Especially important or controversial manuscripts are considered by a group of experienced editors in the chief editorial office, or by an even larger meeting of publishing-house staff.[15] Material drawn from the work of Party organisations must be checked with those organisations before the work is sent to the printer.

Orders placed with the book trade for social and political publications are high (although no statement has been found of the proportion of orders from individuals and organisations respectively). Orders worth 118 million roubles were placed for such material from the publishing-houses' 1975 plans.[16] Certain types of publication, moreover, which are intended for especially wide dissemination (political pamphlets, and important Party and government statements) do not have their edition sizes assessed in the light of pre-publication orders, but are simply 'published in sufficient numbers to satisfy the demands of the population',[17] thus bearing out the director of Politizdat, who, having posed the question of how reader demand was reconciled with Party instructions on the amount of political literature to be issued, replied that the former was expressed by the latter.[18] This practice is probably the most significant cause of the relatively high proportion of unsaleable copies among social and political literature in book trade stocks. In 1974 this proportion was 3.6 per cent of books on political economy and 3.2 per cent of those on scientific communism, compared with an average of 1.4 per cent for central publishers' output as a whole.[19] This is confirmed by an analysis of slow-selling and unsaleable books in a sample of 210 bookshops in the RSFSR in May 1974, which stated that a major proportion of such books in the political and socio-economic fields were not sold because more had been delivered than had been ordered.[20]

The transfer of publishing-houses to the new planning and incentive system was expected to bring about a fall in the production of social and political literature, since it was less profitable to the publisher than certain other types of book. It was claimed that the opposite occurred, and that the rate of growth for this type of literature was in fact higher than for other types after the transfer, with the production of Marxist–Leninist classics increasing threefold between 1965 and 1972. If applied to all literature on political and social topics, however, the claim is not substantiated by Soviet publishing statistics. The central publishing-houses handling this literature showed a slight fall in copies issued between 1971 and 1974, compared with a rise recorded by central houses issuing fiction and scientific literature; and the total number of copies of mass political literature published annually fell by 12 per cent between 1971 and 1975.[21]

9.4. *Textbooks*

'Textbooks' is used here to cover *uchebniki* (officially approved textbooks for specific courses) and *uchebnye posobiya* (works approved as supplementary reading). In 1975, textbooks for all levels of education accounted for 23.8 per cent of all copies of books issued in the USSR, and for 34.1 per cent of the paper consumed in book publishing (in printed sheet-copies).[22] Although publishing-houses in the RSFSR produce nearly all the Soviet Union's Russian-language school textbooks (primarily Prosveshchenie, which publishes over 230 million book copies annually), the peripheral republics' commitment to producing textbooks for their own nationalities results, in some cases, in a far higher proportion of paper being used for this purpose than the national average. School textbooks consumed over 50 per cent of the paper allocation to publishers in the Kazakh SSR in 1971,[23] and the Uzbek SSR's publishing system allotted over 70 per cent of paper for book production in 1972 to the Ukituvchi ('Teacher') publishing-house for textbooks.[24]

These figures are a sign of the very high priority given to ensuring that school (and, to a slightly lesser extent, other) textbooks are supplied in adequate numbers to meet course requirements. The forecast number of pupils in each school year is used as the starting point in calculating demand, although the complaint has been made that the educational authorities hamper publishers' plans by repeated revisions of their forecasts. Edition sizes are usually fixed by *tirazhnye komissii*, consisting of representatives of the appropriate State Committee for Publishing, educational ministries, the book trade, and the publishing-house. It is an accepted principle that *all* foreseen demands, at least for school course textbooks, should be met.[25] Indeed, the latter are now the only type of book issued in large editions for which this principle still holds. The persistent under-supply of textbooks for higher and technical education was noted in a joint decree of the CPSU Central Committee and the USSR Council of Ministers in 1966, which permitted the major higher educational institutions, as an exception, to publish their own instructional material to assist in overcoming the shortage. Even by 1974, only 60 or 70 per cent of orders to library supply agencies from institutions of higher and secondary special education were being met.[26]

In the planning and issue of textbooks, the publishing-houses work in close association with the union and republic education ministries, which prepare five-year publication plans for the text-books to support all existing and proposed courses.[27] In working to these plans, publishers will normally commission authors to write textbooks for the specific courses required by the ministries, with the incentive of competitions for the best examples, offering prizes of up to 5000r. For supplementary textbooks, rather more recourse is had to proposals initiated by authors, although such proposals must be approved by the appropriate education ministry on the publishing-house's recommendation.

At least two external referees' reports must be obtained by the publishing-house for manuscripts of textbooks before an education ministry will consider granting formal approval for the textbook to be published for use in a particular course of study. One report must be the work of a specialist of high standing in the subject concerned, and another must be made 'collectively' by a group of specialists in, for example, a university department. The choice of referees must be confirmed by the education ministry from which approval for the textbook is sought. In the case of university text-books it is the usual practice, in addition, for separate chapters or entire manuscripts to be considered at meetings of university staff, and for preliminary reports to be obtained from staff in the author's faculty who have not taken part in writing the work, before the manuscript is sent to the publisher. The norms for editorial work by publishing-house staff on the manuscripts of textbooks allow more editorial time to be spent on them (and also on mass political and popular scientific works) than on any other type of material: between 3 and 4.5 publisher's sheets per month for school textbooks, 4 sheets per month for 'mass' publications, and between 5 and 9 sheets per month for higher education textbooks.[28]

A textbook manuscript finally presented by the publisher to an education ministry for its confirmation (*grif*) may then be sent by the ministry for further opinions if there is a divergence of views among the original referees. Criticism after publication may cause the *grif* to be withdrawn: after A. E. Furman's textbook *Dialekticheskaya kontseptsiya razvitiya sovremennoi biologii* (*The dialectical conception of the development of modern biology*, published by Vysshaya Shkola in 1974) had been attacked in the Party journal *Kommunist* for 'disorienting students in their evaluation of erroneous concepts that have been rejected', the USSR Ministry of Higher and Secondary Special Education issued an order withdrawing its *grif* from the work (and thus the permission for it to be used in university courses), and instructing its department of social science teaching to intensify supervision of the literature for which it was responsible.[29] An education ministry's *grif* is required before the author may receive his fee, which is paid in addition to his salary even where a textbook has been prepared in the course of his employment. The fee is paid on the basis of the length of the work agreed in the contract, not the published length, as is the case for other types of book. Some concern has been expressed over a tendency to inflate the size of textbooks. Nearly one quarter of a sample reported on by the State Committee for Publishing in 1973 were found to be 'too long',[30] and a special commission was set up in 1975 to reduce the average size by fixing maximum lengths.

The economics of textbook publishing are affected by the very low retail prices set for all such material; the enormous edition sizes and multiple reissuing required for some titles in contrast with the small printings for some national minorities; and the frequent textual alterations demanded that necessitate new editions or entirely new books.

A complete set of course textbooks in Russian for the first to the tenth class, eighty-four titles in all, was said in 1972 to have a total retail price of 28.18r., an average of only 33k. per book. At the same time, textbooks published in Russian, Ukrainian and Uzbek were said to be the only ones which, overall, avoided making a loss;

and total losses incurred by textbooks were given as 5.4 million roubles annually.[31] The director-general of the Vyshcha Shkola publishing association in the Ukrainian SSR claimed in 1975 that prices for textbooks in higher education would need to be raised from the existing 2.2–2.8k. per publisher's sheet to 3.5–4.0k. per sheet to produce an adequate profit.[32] By contrast, Prosveshchenie, the principal publisher of school textbooks in Russian, issues them in an average edition size of two million copies, and in 1974 made a profit of 14.8 million roubles from sales of about 95 million roubles (at retail prices), even after bearing losses of 4.3 million roubles from textbooks in colour, which are adversely affected by the price structure.[33] Standard literary texts and collections of extracts, which demand no outlay on authors' fees once the period of copyright protection has expired, are important contributors to the profitability of textbook publishing. Considerable profit is also derived from reissues, which are undertaken far more frequently for textbooks than for any other type of work: the five-year plan of Prosveshchenie for 1971–5 contained 2011 new titles and 1455 reissues.

A substantial change in the policy of textbook provision was initiated with the introduction of a revised school syllabus, beginning in 1966, accompanied by a new generation of 'stable' (*stabil'nye*) textbooks, which were intended to remain valid for longer periods than previously. By the end of 1975, Prosveshchenie had prepared 103 textbooks for the new syllabus, of which 90 had been confirmed as stable.[34] Quality in stable textbooks has been encouraged by a decree of the USSR Council of Ministers which introduced double fees for the authors of approved stable course textbooks for all-union use. The same decree also provided for the establishment of school libraries from which stable textbooks could be issued to pupils and returned at the end of each school year, as in state schools in Britain, and in contrast with the prevailing Soviet practice under which each child, or its parents, has to buy a set of textbooks for each year. This practice had given rise to a highly organised trade in textbooks at the end of each school year, when some 125 million copies changed hands through the state book trade and the consumer cooperatives. The smaller republics have been the first to introduce school libraries on a large scale. The Estonian SSR was supplying all pupils in eight-year schools by this means in 1974 (having called upon voluntary contributions to supplement state funds for the outlay required), and was counting upon the longer active life of the textbooks to free paper and printing capacity which could be used to issue more profitable publications.[35]

9.5. *Scientific and technical works*

The Russian term *nauchno-tekhnicheskaya literatura* is applied on occasions to all scholarly and technical works, but is most frequently used to designate 'scientific and technical' publications as they are understood in English. Of 'scholarly' (*nauchnye*) books and pamphlets issued in 1975, 72.4 per cent of volumes dealt with subjects in the natural sciences, mathematics, technology, agriculture or medicine. 66.5 per cent of all non-fictional volumes (including popular works, official publications and textbooks) treated topics in the same fields.[36] The small and highly specialised readership for many of these works is reflected in the very low average edition sizes for scholarly scientific and technical publications, which fell from 5100 copies to 1800 copies between 1955 and 1969, and to 1416 copies in 1975.[37] A shortage of paper may have been allowed to exert a particularly strong influence on the reduction of edition sizes for these works *because of* a generally accepted increase in specialisation. Satisfaction rates reported by the RSFSR book trade in 1975 were much higher for scientific and technical literature, at 57 per cent, than for fiction and children's books, and reached 75 per cent for agriculture;[38] but a survey of demand for scientific and technical literature, carried out by Soyuzkniga and reported in 1972, found that only 13.4 per cent of the specialists asked said that they could obtain from bookshops all the books they needed; 64.3 per cent were able to buy some of their requirements, and 22.1 per cent none at all.[39]

With such low edition sizes, many scientific and technical publications bring a loss to the publisher, despite the provision in the retail pricing structure allowing the price of small-edition scholarly works to be raised as high as 15k. per publisher's sheet in order to avoid a loss. Three-quarters of the books and pamphlets issued by scientific and technical publishers were making a loss in 1974,[40] although all the central houses publishing this type of material were said in 1975 to be profitable, probably thanks to the effect of technical titles intended for large readerships and issued in substantial edition sizes. Delays in editorial and production processes affect the topicality, and hence the saleability, of scientific and technical publications especially sharply. A check of book trade stocks in

1973 showed that scientific and technical literature composed 36.7 per cent of all copies regarded as unsaleable, although it formed only about 23 per cent of all book copies reaching the book trade.[41]

In 1975 the State Committee for Publishing began a new approach to the problem of setting accurate edition sizes for highly specialised works. A limited number of publishers were allowed to announce such works in their annual publication plans with a guarantee that all pre-publication orders would be met, since the edition size (usually not more than 1500) would be fixed on the basis of those orders only.[42]

Increasing specialisation in science and technology, and the lengthy gestation times suffered by books in publishing-houses, have had the further effect of making publication by institutions and universities of their own research a more attractive means of disseminating results to a limited readership. This publishing activity, and the rapid growth in the output of scientific and technical information centres in many branches of industry, has been described as the rise of a separate Soviet publishing system, parallel to the established scientific and technical publishing-houses.[43] Publishing activity other than by publishing-houses has been the subject of many attempts at strict regulation (as described in 9.8), and efforts have been made to channel some of the material contained in institutions' own *sborniki* and *nauchnye trudy* into scholarly journals. The USSR Academy of Sciences stopped the publication by its institutions of about 400 such irregular series during the 1960s, and it was claimed that this made possible the establishment of eighty-two new scholarly journals.[44] Steps have also been taken to divert highly specialised research reports away from the traditional publishing process altogether, by registering and depositing them at information centres from which copies can be supplied on request.

9.6. *Children's books*

Publications for children (excluding school textbooks) are issued by at least a third of the publishing-houses in the USSR, but the pre-eminent house in this field is Detskaya Literatura, which published 223.6 million of the 448.7 million copies of children's books which appeared in 1975.[45] A CPSU Central Committee decree in 1969 drew attention to the insufficient quantity, and sometimes poor quality, of children's literature, and ordered a general improvement by publishing-houses in both respects, but despite an increase in edition sizes supplies have remained inadequate. The satisfaction level in the RSFSR book trade was reported as 22 per cent in 1975 – not much higher than the 16.8 per cent reported for adult fiction.[46] This was notwithstanding the plans of the RSFSR State Committee for Publishing (which administers a high proportion of houses publishing children's books, including Detskaya Literatura) to increase the number of copies of children's books issued by 40 per cent during the plan period 1971–5, compared with an overall growth of book copies published for the republic over that period of 9.9 per cent.[47] Production of children's literature in some of the peripheral republics has been stated to be particularly inadequate. In 1974, less than one copy of a children's book for every child aged from three to seventeen was published in the Kirghiz, Tadzhik, Kazakh, Uzbek and Azerbaidzhan SSRs, compared with nine copies per head in the RSFSR and eight in the Estonian SSR.[48]

Schools and libraries receive a large share of the children's books published. A delegation of American publishers was told in 1970 that about 50 per cent of children's literature went to schools and libraries, and about 10 per cent was exported.[49] In 1975 the State Committee for Publishing approved plans for a fifty-volume series, *Biblioteka mirovoi literatury dlya detei* (*Library of world literature for children*), each volume to be published by Detskaya Literatura in 400 000 copies, of which half would be sold on subscription to school libraries.

9.7. Books for libraries

The supply of books to libraries is regarded as an important element in book distribution, not only because of the educational and ideological functions ascribed to Soviet libraries, but also because libraries are seen as an effective means of making books available – in conditions of shortage – to as many as possible of those who wish to read them. One hundred million roubles is said to be spent annually on books for libraries open to the general public;[50] although research carried out in 1969–71 found that in some smaller libraries 40 per cent of books received in 1968–9 on pre-Revolutionary Russian history had not been read, nor had 35 per cent on the life and literature of foreign countries, nor 34 per cent on morals and upbringing.[51] This may have been the ground for the assertion, made by a senior official of the State Committee for Publishing in

1975, that public libraries were spending 40 million roubles a year on books which were not in demand.[52]

Libraries as a whole in the USSR purchase about 20 per cent of the book trade's annual turnover. Approximately half this proportion is acquired through the library supply agencies (*bibliotechnye kollektory*) in Glavkniga's trading organisation.[53] These agencies work under contracts with libraries, usually on an annual basis, to supply titles ordered by them up to a specified expenditure limit, often with a percentage breakdown by subject. Smaller public libraries are obliged to spend a minimum proportion (50–60 per cent) of their book funds in transactions with the library supply agencies. There have been frequent complaints of supply agencies' slowness in procuring publications, and of their inability to fill many orders because the trading organisations serving them have given priority to retail orders from bookshops.

Beginning in 1973, a more distinct priority has been given to library book provision by the introduction of editions for libraries only. Works are recommended for publication in library editions by the USSR Ministry of Culture, and are supposed to be sold only through library supply agencies, although there have been complaints that some book trade organisations have been selling copies over the counter. In 1975, ninety library editions, totalling 9 million copies, were planned for issue from the central publishers, and 250 more from other houses.[54] Children's books and fiction are receiving the greatest emphasis: the four major houses producing the most titles in library editions in 1974 and 1975 were Detskaya Literatura, Sovetskii Pisatel', Molodaya Gvardiya and Khudozhestvennaya Literatura. Libraries are also being given priority in the supply of popular books not specifically produced for them. The percentage of fiction among publications handled by the RSFSR book trade as a whole in 1974 was 11.6, but in the republic's library supply agencies (which are part of the same trading organisation) the percentage was 24.2.[55] Cases have also been quoted of entire editions of multi-volume works, already announced for subscription, being diverted to libraries.[56]

9.8. *Works issued by organisations other than publishing-houses*

Publications issued by bodies which are not themselves publishing-houses can be divided into those which are published by organisations which have themselves been granted a more or less restricted right to issue printed matter (or which, in some cases, have simply ignored the requirement that such a right must be granted); and 'commissioned' publications, which are issued by regular publishers on behalf, and at the expense, of another organisation.

The question of the extent to which bodies other than publishing-houses should be allowed to issue printed matter has exercised Party and government authorities at intervals for many years. This has been partly because of the difficulty of controlling the content of such publications, but also because of a persistent tendency for increasing numbers of organisations to issue ever larger amounts of material. A Central Committee decree of 1970 which was intended to reduce this type of publishing activity (because of the ineffectiveness of a 1966 decree with the same purpose) pointed out that books and pamphlets issued by bodies other than publishing-houses had composed 35 per cent of volumes issued in 1966, and had grown to 47.6 per cent at the time of the decree.[57] The decree ordered a thorough revision of the list of organisations with publishing rights, and stricter regulation of the types of material which bodies retaining those rights were allowed to issue. The same decree ordered a large-scale introduction of deposit, instead of publication, for research reports, to reduce the need for small-edition scholarly publications.

The ensuing regulations, produced by the (then) Committee for the Press in 1971,[58] allowed the main higher educational institutions and research institutes to publish collections of articles (*sborniki*) on special subjects, and (in the case of some institutions) highly-specialised textbooks. With these exceptions, educational and research institutions, government departments, creative unions, societies and other organisations – provided they had been granted publishing rights – were allowed to produce only printed matter regarded as being for internal use, such as regulations, price-lists, thesis summaries, auxiliary teaching materials and departmental statistics. All other publications were to be issued as 'commissioned' publications by a publishing-house, except for scientific and technical information publications, which were to be produced under plans approved by the State Committee for Science and Technology. Organisations' publishing plans were to be subject to the approval of the appropriate Committee for the Press, which had the right to demand any manuscripts or referees' reports when considering such plans, and to set limits on the amount of matter to be issued.

The revised list of organisations with publishing rights reduced their number (excluding government departments) from 2904 in 1970 to 623 in 1972,[59] but it was still being claimed in that year that organisations were taking advantage of those rights to issue publications of general interest in order to make a profit. Instances given included a football calendar issued by an industrial combine in Maikop, and a book on the railways of the Smolensk *oblast'*, by the local branch of the Union of Journalists.[60]

The erratically varied contents of *sborniki* published by universities and other institutions had received much unfavourable comment, because useful contributions were difficult to trace in them and the mixture of subjects made many of them unsaleable. The Moscow State Pedagogical Institute was said in 1971 to have accumulated unsold publications to the value of 100 000 roubles.[61] The Central Committee decree of 1970, put into effect by an order of the USSR Ministry of Higher and Secondary Special Education in the following year, prohibited the further publication of unspecialised *sborniki*. A further order in 1975 (by which time the number of educational institutions with publishing rights had grown yet again from 262 in 1967 to 374) strengthened the Ministry's powers of supervision over the content and planning of publications issued by educational institutions.[62]

Despite all these measures, the attraction to organisations of issuing their own publications remains a strong one, owing at least as much to the delays which they experience in their dealings with publishing-houses as to considerations of prestige. In 1971, the year after the Central Committee decree on the matter, books and pamphlets not issued by publishing-houses accounted for 46 per cent of volumes issued, though only for 5.2 per cent of the number of copies and 2.1 per cent of the paper, as measured in printed sheet-copies. In 1974 the equivalent figures had increased again slightly, to 47 per cent of the volumes, 6.9 per cent of the copies and 2.6 per cent of the paper; but figures for 1975 showed a fall to 44.6 per cent of volumes, 4.7 per cent of copies and 2.1 per cent of paper.[63] The State Committee for Publishing began another effort in 1975 to reduce the number of bodies with publishing rights, this time accompanied by limits on the length and edition size of their publications: *sborniki* were restricted to a maximum of ten sheets and 1000 copies, and specialised textbooks to five sheets and 1500 copies; and the target was set of a 30–35 per cent reduction in the average length of all such publications.[64]

'Commissioned' publications (*zakaznye izdaniya*), issued by a publishing-house under contract on behalf of another organisation, must be 'coordinated' as regards content in the usual way, and must be included in the publisher's planning procedures and his requests for printing capacity. The organisation placing the order is responsible for obtaining permission for the supply of the necessary paper, and must cover the publisher's entire outlay, including a 5 per cent profit calculated on total costs.[65] Although publishers are instructed to accept orders only for books appropriate to their own 'profile' and to the nature of the commissioning organisation, some commissioned books continue to appear for reasons primarily of profit or prestige. An especially flagrant example, which was publicised as a warning to others in 1975, was the 454-page souvenir volume *Zemlya nasha lipetsskaya* (*Our country of Lipetsk*), published in 23 000 copies in 1974 by the Tsentral'no-Chernozemnoe publishing-house. It was issued on the orders of the Lipetsk Party district committee, which obtained for it the necessary fifty tons of scarce offset paper (the same amount as was allocated to the publisher for an entire year's output of children's books).[66] Subsequent efforts to dispose of surplus copies included their unsolicited despatch to foreign libraries as exchange material.

9.9. *Works translated from foreign languages*

Until the USSR adhered to the Universal Copyright Convention (UCC) in 1973, the translation by Soviet publishing-houses of books from foreign countries was the subject of international copyright protection only in the few instances where the countries concerned had concluded bilateral copyright agreements with the USSR, although agreements on the translation of individual works could be, and often were, concluded. The Soviet legislation introduced in 1973 to conform to the requirements of the UCC now lays down, however, that any translation, and any subsequent publication of it, may normally be made only with the permission of the author or his assign, subject to payment and under conditions stipulated in a contract, for the duration of the period of copyright protection.

Because, presumably, of these requirements and the consequent frequent need to pay a fee in foreign currency for translation rights, the number of books and pamphlets translated from foreign languages and published in the USSR has fallen from 2639 volumes in 1971 to 1627 in 1975.[67] A trend towards selecting a wider range of modern Western fiction for translation has been tentatively identified, with much of the initiative for this arising among editorial staff in the publishing-houses concerned,[68] but there is so far no evidence of an increase in the number of copies of translations issued.

The importance of careful and vigilant selection by Soviet publishers in choosing works for translation from foreign languages has been frequently stressed by Party and government, and is visible in a number of special regulations applying to the publication of translations.[69] A publishing-house considering translation of a foreign work must, unless there is a special need for speedy publication, obtain at least two recommendations for the translation from scholarly institutions or specialists, and secure the agreement of the appropriate chief editorial office in the State Committee for Publishing before submitting details of the work for 'coordination' to the State Committee or (in the case of scientific and technical works) to the State Scientific and Technical Library. The choice of translators, and of authors to write any notes or introduction to the work, must be approved by a senior editor or the head of an editorial office.

An annual combined plan for the issue of works translated from foreign languages is prepared by the State Committee for Publishing, working from publishers' editorial preparation plans. The Writers' Union, the Gor'kii Institute of World Literature, the State Library for Foreign Literature, and the publishing-houses Mir and Progress (which are the main producers of translated works) are all called upon for assessment of the combined plan. Translations now protected under the UCC (for which a fee, often in foreign currency, is normally payable, and for which higher retail prices are allowed in the case of fiction) must be incorporated into a separate special plan approved by the State Committee for Publishing.[70] These protracted approval processes have drawn the complaint that they are delaying the appearance, and hence reducing the usefulness, of many works, particularly scientific and technical translations, by prolonging their preparation time to as much as five years.[71]

9.10. *Forecasting demand and output for different types of publication*

Soviet forecasts of demand and output for different types of publication provide a useful extra dimension to two recurring themes in this chapter: the shortfalls in the production of many kinds of literature, and the priorities observed in reducing them. The All-Union Research Institute for Complex Polygraphic Problems is heading a series of forecasting projects by several institutions, and is itself undertaking a fundamental study of factors affecting demand and output up to the year 2000. This project is examining the likely effects of changes in the role of book publishing as one of several means of mass communication; changes in the composition and requirements of the reading public arising from more free time and improved educational standards; and foreseeable alterations in the structure of special types of literature as a result of, for example, increasing scientific specialisation and the growth of school libraries.[72]

TABLE 3. *Soviet demand and output forecasts for*
books and pamphlets, 1980 and 1990 (millions of copies)

	1972 actual[a]	1975 actual[b]	1980 ideal[c]	1990 (1973 forecast)[d] Multiple of 1972 in brackets[e]	
Mass political literature	151.3	161.8	381.0	181.6–226.9	(1.2–1.5)
Scholarly literature	27.9	35.7	63.0	41.8	(1.5)
Popular scientific literature	66.4	77.9	476.0	99.6–132.8	(1.5–2.0)
Production and related instructional literature	191.1	176.0	306.0	NDA	(up to 3.0)[f]
Adult fiction	176.3	221.9	698.0	528.9	(3.0)
Children's books (excluding textbooks)	363.7	448.7	775.0	727.4–909.2	(2.0–2.5)
Reference works	44.1	51.0	280.0	52.9–61.7	(1.2–1.4)
Totals	1020.8	1173.0	2979.0		

Sources and notes
a. *Pechat' SSSR v 1972 godu*, pp. 24–5, 27.
b. *Pechat' SSSR v 1975 godu*, pp. 40–4.
c. *Voprosy ekonomiki i organizatsii truda v poligrafii* (M., 1971), pp. 3–18.
d. 'O tendentsiyakh vypuska osnovnykh vidov knizhnoi produktsii do 1990g.' *Izd. delo. Ref. inf.*, 1973(5), 8–11.
e. The forecasts in the source are given as multiples of output in an unstated base year, which has been assumed to be 1972 – the latest complete year for which figures would have been available. The absolute figures in this column are calculated from the 1972 output on this assumption. An earlier base year would, of course, yield lower absolute figures.
f. The greatest increase is expected in 'domestic' publications (books on housekeeping, cookery, fashion, etc.).

The All-Union Book Chamber has embarked upon a comple-mentary project to forecast the production of books in greater detail up to 1990.[73] This work appears to have succeeded an earlier and cruder study, completed by 1971 and making projections for the period up to 1980,[74] which relied upon demographic trends and evidence of reader demand furnished by the book trade, in con-junction with highly optimistic expectations of paper supply, to forecast the minimum number of copies needed to 'remove the discrepancy between supply and demand' by 1980. The second forecast (to 1990) has produced more modest preliminary figures which envisage a much slower rate of growth over the longer period. Placed in comparison with what may be termed the 'ideal' pro-jections for 1980 (as shown in table 3), the 1990 forecast points up the anticipated amount of unsatisfied demand for several types of literature as far ahead as that date.

It will be noted that the 1990 forecast expects the greatest in-creases in supply to be in recreational publications: adult fiction and 'domestic' publications, followed by children's books and popular scientific works. The slowest growth is expected in mass political literature, and – interestingly – in reference works, where the pro-jection for 1980 saw the second largest proportional increase as desirable. Policy decisions since 1973 have, if anything, increased the priority granted to adult fiction (as recounted in 9.2) at the expense of some varieties of mass political literature, the over-supply of which is now recognised (see 9.3).

10

Conclusions

Publishing policies, in the USSR as elsewhere, are not necessarily either consistent or coherent. Issues rise to the surface for discussion and decision as a result of complex pressures and of circumstances which are by no means all open to observation. Subject to these unavoidable obstacles in the way of a precise or complete picture, conclusions from the evidence presented in this book are expressed here as the outcome of the intention declared in chapter 1: to show the effects of the interaction between the special characteristics of publishing and some distinctive features of Soviet society; and to illustrate their impact on the books which appear in the USSR.

Western descriptions of Soviet publishing policy have tended to emphasise the Soviet view of publishing as a tool of social and ideological influence; the unchallenging observance of directives from superior authority; and the subordination of economic considerations to political imperatives in the industry's management. The evidence presented in this book indicates that these matters of emphasis, while certainly elements in Soviet publishing policy, are misleading if over-stressed or taken in isolation.

Soviet publishing administrators work within an industrial system which is less open to radical manipulation than the accepted Western view suggests. Certainly the assumption prevails among Soviet policy-makers that the production of books is a laudable undertaking, which is of ideological, cultural, scientific and (possibly) directly economic benefit provided that the content of the books concerned has been approved as acceptable; and the consequent further assumption is made that production of acceptable books should be maintained at least at the present level, and increased if possible, since there are clear symptoms of unsatisfied demand for nearly all categories of publication. It seems to have been less remarked, however, that these assumptions are reinforced by the scale of the publishing–printing–bookselling sector itself, and by the features characteristic of Soviet society which have rendered publishing a self-justifying industry with a strongly traditional outlook. A firmly established, centrally controlled manufacturing and distri-

122

butive undertaking (with over 300 000 staff and producing – in books alone – over 80 000 different new products annually with a total retail value of over 750 million roubles) will be little inclined to question, or to have questioned, either its status as an institution or the purpose of its activities: the less so since that status is preserved by the position of its senior administration as a high-ranking component of government, and since the standard industrial planning routines foster the inclination to aim each year at quantitative improvement rather than qualitative innovation, except by direct intervention from above.

This essentially traditional view of publishing becomes more evident when one examines the way in which a Soviet book's contribution to a socialist society is assessed. A publishing industry which claims to be issuing books to produce specific social impacts, rather than in order to make the maximum profit, might be expected to have given serious attention to evaluating the effect of books in the hands of their ultimate users. In fact, Soviet research on reading habits and the sociology of the book has rarely been applied to this kind of assessment,[1] and by far the most common criteria for judging a book's 'success' are two of those applied by capitalist publishers: the number of copies printed and sold, and the work's critical reception. The lower status enjoyed in the USSR by the capitalist publisher's third success indicator – profit – serves to emphasise that a publishing operation which issues only those works authoritatively passed as suitable for their intended readership will tend to measure its performance by the number of such works it produces and the nature of the authoritative criticism which they evoke.

The large industrial and economic scale of publishing has also affected Soviet views on the availability and pricing of books. Pressure for books to be supplied to the public at less than cost price was overridden with the introduction of the New Economic Policy in 1921, but the principles of maximum access and economic viability have coexisted uneasily ever since. It could well be argued that the incompatibility between economic and ideological preferences has been at least partially resolved, now that much of Soviet publishing is showing itself to be profitable. A change in publishing priorities could no doubt render it even more profitable, despite the present paper shortage; but the forces opposed to the profit motive are more powerful than in Western publishing, and include considerations which are scholarly and literary, as well as political. The

Soviet administration's present view is that the current, relatively small, subsidies for publishing activity should be reduced wherever this can be achieved by greater efficiency, but not by means of unacceptable price increases, nor by unacceptable changes in the assortment or number of copies of each type of literature.

'Acceptability' in these matters has been and remains a variable quality. It can be affected by pressures, as is made evident by the recent decisions to reduce the priority given to periodicals and increase that given to fiction. The pressures are often themselves conflicting, stemming as they do from sectional interests, from the interpretation of readers' demands, and from convictions about readers' needs and the formation of tastes. They are exerted by publishers, the book trade, the printing industry, and the Writers' Union (though in all likelihood rarely against the views of the Party element at the points concerned), as well as by rulings stemming from internal debates in Party and government. Less directly, pressure is exerted by authors' willingness to write on given topics, and by the power of individual readers to swell subscription lists, to influence orders from libraries, or in the last resort to leave thousands of books unbought.

Such pressures to produce variations in the acceptability of policy options are exerted within limits of another kind which are much less open to question or re-negotiation. These constraints are, firstly, that of total available paper supplies and printing capacity; and secondly, the insistence on the revocable 'right to publish' and on the principle of regulating from the centre the output of all organs issuing printed matter. The two together have inevitably led to the need for a massive allocational procedure each year to link publishers, printers and material stocks; and to guide this procedure the administrative imposition of priorities for different types of literature has become a necessity because of an unwillingness to determine priorities from 'raw' demand (although a degree of response to demand is admitted), and because of reluctance to manipulate demand through the pricing structure.

These priorities in ranking different types of literature become visible in the efforts to maintain or achieve full satisfaction, or even saturation, of requirements for books with the highest priority, and in the relative importance attached to increasing the supply of other types of work, to which greater or lesser limitations on paper consumption must be applied. The slow growth in paper production is likely to force the retention of such limitations and their accompanying priority system for the foreseeable future – not only between different types of book, but between books, journals, newspapers and other kinds of printed matter – and the existing incentives to conserve paper may be expected to continue, and even increase.

A different set of constraints applies to policy over *what* is published (as distinct from how much). At any one time, many topics and many manners of treatment are not accepted for public circulation in the Soviet media. The boundaries of the admissible vary with time and place, and may not be uniformly enforced in the same place at the same time; but in the case of every work considered for publication a series of decisions is made on its ideological and political acceptability, as well as on its literary or scholarly quality: initially by the author himself before writing or submitting the work, and subsequently by publishing-house editorial staff, often by the house's external referees and its superior organisation, often by the Writers' Union (if it is a work of fiction), nearly always by the State Committee for Publishing, and nearly always by the censorship.

The quite rigid demarcation of subject or other specialities between publishing-houses introduces a further constraint into the composition of Soviet book production. It leads to lack of manoeuvrability in reacting in print to new topics because of the long advance planning period needed to lay down the number of titles and copies to be issued by each house in each year, and at the same time restricts an author's scope for choosing an outlet for his work. Although publishing-houses' output is intended to be adjusted to the book trade's requirements through the system of pre-publication ordering, in recent years this has no longer held good for the bulk of books intended for the general reader, due to the under-supply of fiction and children's books and the over-supply of some types of mass political literature.

The ultimate foci for most pressures for change in the acceptability of policy options are the Central Committee's Department of Propaganda and the State Committee for Publishing, which between them hold most of the effective power to enforce or stimulate observance of major changes in policy by publishers, printers and booksellers; to provide incentives for more or better-quality works in a particular field; and to inhibit or forbid undesirable phenomena such as excessive length or duplication of treatment. The Department of Propaganda, through Glavlit, also retains the ultimate negative sanction of censorship.

The individual Soviet publishing-house is obliged to follow policy determined by higher authority on many matters affecting its operations, and in the opposite direction has to transmit to its superiors pressures and initiatives, or conduct negotiations, on matters about which it cannot take the final decision. It nevertheless retains some discretion to commission, reject and accept manuscripts, subject to final approval by its superiors; and the majority of titles issued by most Soviet publishing-houses result from their exercise of this discretion, and not from the assignment to them of works which they are instructed to publish. 'Overall' publication plans, compiled nationally by the central state publishing administration, remain in large measure the sum of individual houses' own plans. The Soviet publishing-house therefore retains the publisher's traditional position as the principal agency which identifies the need for publications and secures authors to provide them. Higher administrations have (in some cases consciously) withstood the temptation to remove these functions from the publishing-houses, and they remain the houses' most distinctive characteristic.

It is probably this surviving scope for initiative (circumscribed though it is by the house's 'profile', the State Committee's coordination procedures, and the bounds of the politically admissible) which is the foundation of the Soviet publishing-house's remaining sense of identity. It is among editorial staff in the publishing-house that a willingness to take initiatives – and indeed to bear certain risks – is more frequently found than at other points in the publishing process. Although far from universal even among editors, this willingness is part of a persisting concern that a house should earn a reputation through the quality of its publications – a concern which is patent to the foreign visitor among many Soviet publishing staff.

Appendix 1. Authors' fee scales

The scales below were introduced for the RSFSR in 1975, and are taken from *Sobranie postanovleniya pravitel'stva RSFSR*, 1975(9), 148–57, 163–6. The exact fee paid is fixed by negotiation at the maximum or minimum point, or at one of a number of stated points within the range (not shown below). Amounts are in roubles per author's sheet.

A. ORIGINAL WORKS OF IMAGINATIVE LITERATURE AND ASSOCIATED WRITING

Normal edition sizes

Prose fiction (including works for children), plays, film scripts	150–400
Short stories of up to one sheet (for the entire work)	150–400
One-act plays (for the entire work)	200–600
Prose work based on folk literature	100–200
Poetry (per line)	0.7–2.0
Poems of up to thirty lines (for the entire work)	30–200
Works of literature re-told for children	75–200
Popular scientific literature for children	150–300
Literary history and criticism	150–400
Original bibliographical works, chronologies	120–200
Commentaries and notes	50–200
Introductory chapters, prefaces, conclusions	200–600

Mass edition sizes

Prose fiction (including works for children), plays, film scripts	250–400
Prose work based on folk literature	150–200
Poetry (per line)	1.4–2.0
Works of literature re-told for children	100–200
Popular scientific literature for children	200–300
Literary history and criticism	250–400
Prose works in the series *Shkol'naya biblioteka*	250–400

B. ORIGINAL WORKS OF POLITICAL, SCIENTIFIC, TECHNICAL, INSTRUCTIONAL AND OTHER LITERATURE

Monographs on theoretical and scientific topics	150–300
(over 50 000 copies: +50%; over 100 000 copies: +75%)	
Mass political literature	150–300
(over 100 000 copies: +50%; over 200 000: +75%.	
Above five sheets, only one-quarter of the fee is paid)	
Mass political pamphlets of up to four sheets (for the entire work)	up to 1600
Popular scientific literature (except for children)	100–300
(over 100 000 copies: +50%; over 200 000 copies: +75%.	
Above ten sheets, only one-quarter of the fee is paid)	
Works on production and technology; scientific, technical and other reference works, statistical compilations, guide books	80–200
Course textbooks for higher educational institutions and for the CPSU and Komsomol educational systems	150–250
(over 750 000 copies: +50%)	
Course textbooks for institutions of secondary special education	100–200
(over 750 000 copies: +50%)	
Textbooks for school children in classes 1–3	100–150
(over 750 000 copies: +50%)	
Textbooks for school children in classes 4–9	100–200
(over 750 000 copies: +50%)	
Works on the methodology and organisation of the educational process. Pedagogical literature for parents	100–150
Encyclopedia and dictionary articles of over 40 000 typographical units	200–350
Explanatory dictionaries; dictionaries of special terms and synonyms	100–300
Lexical and orthographical dictionaries:	
of languages using alphabetic script	80–150
of languages using non-alphabetic script	100–300
Introductory chapters, prefaces and conclusions to other authors' works	150–300
Original bibliographical works, chronologies	40–100
Commentaries and notes	40–120

C. COMPILATION FEES FOR COLLECTIONS OF OTHER AUTHORS'
WORKS

Thematic collections and works of an encyclopedic nature for children	20–80
Chrestomathies of imaginative literature	30–80
Collections of proverbs and sayings	50–150
Collections of non-fictional material involving textual preparation	15–40
Collections of official materials	10–20

D. TRANSLATIONS

Prose fiction (ordinary editions)	50–150
Prose fiction (mass editions)	100–150
Marxist–Leninist classics	50–100
Socio-economic, philosophical, legal, scientific, technical and reference works	40–80
Other works	30–60

Appendix 2. All-union book retail prices

The prices below are taken from 'Preiskurant No. 116' as amended to 1 January 1977 and shown in *Spravochnik normativnykh materialov dlya izdatel'skikh rabotnikov*, 2nd ed. (M., 1977), pp. 110–51. Extracts applying to books and pamphlets only are shown.

Prices are in kopeks per publisher's sheet, and exclude the cost of any form of binding. They apply to works printed on No. 1 (higher-grade) paper, except for categories marked *, where the price applies to works on all grades of paper. Otherwise, works printed on No. 2 and No. 3 paper are priced at 0.3 kopeks per sheet less throughout.

A. SOCIO-POLITICAL LITERATURE

Works of the founders of Marxism–Leninism. Materials of congresses and conferences of the CPSU and Central Committee plenums. Trade-union and Komsomol documents. Collections of works and speeches by Party and government leaders	2.4
Mass official publications. Separate speeches of Party and government leaders. Agitational literature	2.1
Biographies of founders of Marxism–Leninism and of notable political figures. Materials of congresses of communist and workers' parties in foreign countries. Works by figures in the international communist, workers' and national liberation movements	2.6
Mass editions of socio-political literature, reference works and collections of documents. Literature on the work of the Party, trade-union, Komsomol and pioneer organisations	2.6
Popular scientific works, memoirs, travel accounts, journalists' notes	3.2
Collections of archival material and documents for specialists	3.8
Contemporary popular scientific and mass literature on international themes, translated from foreign languages	4.0
Collected works in social and political sciences	4.3

130

Scholarly publications (monographs and *nauchnye trudy* of institutions, including translated works):	
for scholars and specialists	6.3
for a wide circle of readers	3.2
Handbooks, state-of-the-art reviews, instructions and special reference works:	
for specialists	5.3
for mass occupations	3.8

B. Course and supplementary textbooks and educational literature

Course and supplementary textbooks for schools:	
black and white for classes 1–4	1.0*
black and white for classes 5–10	1.3*
in two colours	1.4*
in three or more colours	1.8*
Course and supplementary textbooks for evening and correspondence classes, and for the Party and Komsomol educational systems	2.0*
Course and supplementary textbooks for institutions of secondary special education:	
in socio-political disciplines	2.2*
in basic agricultural disciplines	2.5*
in mathematics, physics, chemistry, foreign languages and other general disciplines	2.7*
in special disciplines	3.3*
for pedagogical and medical colleges	2.3*
Course and supplementary textbooks for higher educational institutions:	
in socio-political disciplines	2.3*
in basic agricultural disciplines	2.7*
in mathematics, physics, chemistry, foreign languages and other general disciplines	2.8*
in special disciplines	3.5*
Course and supplementary textbooks for institutions of higher and secondary special education in art and architecture, printed on superior paper with illustrations	5.0*
Methodological literature on teaching and education.	
Literature for parents	3.0

C. Works on technology and production. Works in the natural, exact and technical sciences, health, medicine, physical culture and sport

Popular scientific literature (biographies of scientists, technologists, organisers of production and outstanding workers, works on scientific discoveries and the propagation of advanced production experience)   3.3

Guides, methodological and practical handbooks, state-of-the-art reviews, technical instructions and other works on production techniques, including translations:

    for engineers, technologists and specialists   5.3
    for foremen and workers   3.8
    for subordinate medical staff   3.0

Special reference works:

    for engineers, technologists, economists, doctors and accountants   5.3
    for foremen and workers   3.8

Standards   5.3

Price-lists   3.3

Contemporary popular scientific literature translated from foreign languages   5.0

Collected and selected works, and editions of separate works, by leading scholars:

    without a large reference apparatus   5.0
    with detailed commentary, preface, or similar apparatus, if published by an Academy of Sciences   7.0

Monographs and other scholarly works   6.3

Collections of articles (*nauchnye trudy*, etc.) from research and higher educational institutions   7.0

Contemporary scientific literature translated from foreign languages   7.2

D. Works on agriculture

Literature propagating advanced production experience, and biographies on the same theme. Works on scientific discoveries. Popular scientific literature   2.8

Methodological and practical handbooks, reference works, instructions, and other production literature, including translations:

    for specialists   4.3
    for mass occupations   3.6

Contemporary popular scientific literature translated from
  foreign languages   5.0

E. WORKS ON HOUSEKEEPING AND TOURISM. MASS HANDBOOKS IN
THE SERVICE SPHERE. PUBLICITY MATERIAL. MASS AND POPULAR
SCIENTIFIC WORKS ON PHYSICAL CULTURE, SPORTS AND PASTIMES

Transport timetables. Telephone and address directories.
  Publicity material. Entry conditions and guides for entrants
  to educational institutions   3.3
Mass literature on tourism and sport. General tourist guides   6.6
Works on domestic economy (dressmaking, household repairs,
  mushroom- and berry-picking, cookery, gardening, bee-
  keeping, rabbit-breeding, home-furnishing, etc.)   7.6
Mass series:
    for radio enthusiasts   7.6
    for photography, cinema, motor-car and aviation
      enthusiasts, and collectors. Collections of crosswords,
      riddles, games   7.6
Guide-books and publicity material with not less than 50%
  of illustrated matter:
    in one or two colours   20.0*
    in three or more colours   32.0*

F. IMAGINATIVE LITERATURE
Prose works:
    contemporary Soviet literature, including translations
      from the national languages of the USSR   6.3
    translations of contemporary foreign writers into
      languages of the USSR. Translations of Soviet writers
      into foreign languages   10.3
    works of other writers. Works of popular creativity   8.3
Poetry:
    contemporary Soviet poetry, including translations from
      the national languages of the USSR   10.3
    translations of contemporary poets into languages of the
      USSR. Translations of Soviet poets into foreign
      languages   10.8
    works of other poets. Popular poetry   8.3
Drama:
    contemporary prose drama   6.3

contemporary verse drama	10.3
classics of world drama	8.3
Prose, poetry, drama, memoirs and letters of foreign writers in foreign languages	10.0
Other memoirs or letters by or dealing with writers. Military memoirs	6.3

Academy editions of literary works, memoirs or letters by or dealing with writers, with a critical apparatus of at least 15% of the total length, edited from original sources:

works of literature, writers' letters and memoirs	10.0
the series *Literaturnye pamyatniki* and *Literaturnoe nasledstvo*	12.0

G. CHILDREN'S LITERATURE

Illustrated books for children of pre-school age	4.5

Illustrated books for younger school-age children:

prose, drama and non-contemporary poetry	3.6
contemporary poetry (including translations)	5.3

Books for older school-age children:

prose, drama and non-contemporary poetry	3.2
contemporary poetry (including translations)	5.3
Illustrated publications in three or more colours for children of all ages	7.1
Biographies, memoirs, travel books, works about occupations, popular scientific literature in all fields	3.2
Illustrated works about writers and artists on superior paper	6.3*

H. WORKS ON LITERARY STUDIES, CRITICISM AND LINGUISTICS

Popular works on Soviet authors	2.8
Contemporary popular works translated from foreign languages	4.0

Works of classic writers:

for specialists, with scholarly apparatus	6.3
for a wide circle of readers	2.8

Scholarly works and monographs:

for specialists	6.3
for a wide circle of readers	4.3

J. WORKS ON BIBLIOGRAPHY, JOURNALISM, PUBLISHING, ARCHIVE AND LIBRARY STUDIES. BIBLIOGRAPHIES

Mass literature for a wide circle of readers	3.3

Scholarly publications	6.3
Reference works, handbooks, technical instructions and similar literature:	
for specialists	5.3
for mass occupations	3.8
Bibliographical reference works	4.3
Methodological guides and similar publications for librarians and archivists	3.0
Recommendatory bibliographies:	
unillustrated	4.3
illustrated	5.3*

K. WORKS ON ART AND CULTURE

Mass series, monographs and reference works. Literature for aesthetic education	3.8
Contemporary literature translated from foreign languages	4.0
Popular works on music	5.0
Guides and practical handbooks for artists	5.0
Scholarly works on the history and theory of the arts and aesthetics. Works on typographical design for specialists. Monographs on artists' and musicians' work	7.0
Memoirs, letters, biographies and travel accounts of artistic and musical figures. Guides to museums, galleries, exhibitions	6.3
Collections of scholarly articles. Reference works for specialists	7.0

L. ENCYCLOPEDIAS AND DICTIONARIES

Universal encyclopedias	5.0*
Popular encyclopedias (medical, household). Specialised encyclopedias and dictionaries in the humanities, general technical disciplines, medicine, agriculture and veterinary science	5.3
Children's encyclopedias	3.0
Specialised encyclopedias and dictionaries in the natural sciences and technology	6.3
Universal encyclopedic dictionaries and reference works	4.3
Dictionaries for Russian and other languages of the USSR for the mass reader	3.3
Bilingual learners' dictionaries of the general literary language, for languages of Europe and the USSR	3.0

Specialist dictionaries for Russian and other languages of the USSR (multi-volume, phraseological, etymological, etc.)	6.0
Bilingual or multilingual specialist dictionaries:	
large (two or more volumes)	7.2
single-volume for a limited readership	7.2
single-volume for a wider readership	4.3
Dictionaries and phrasebooks for foreigners	10.0
Learners' dictionaries on superior paper with coloured illustrations in the text	10.0*
Polytechnical bilingual dictionaries	8.0
Dictionaries for rare or little-known languages, or for languages using hieroglyphic, Arabic or other unusual script	8.0
Specialised bilingual or multilingual technical reference dictionaries	10.0
Small-format dictionaries (1/128 sheet)	10.0

M. Illustrated publications, albums and catalogues. Atlases

Albums, atlases, illustrated scientific, technical and other catalogues:	
in one colour	8.0*
in two colours	10.0*
in three or more colours	16.0*

Albums and art catalogues with specially prepared reproductions:

	on coated paper	on offset or letterpress paper
with monochrome line illustrations	12.0	8.0
as above, with presentation finish	18.0	10.0
with tone illustrations, one or two colours	23.0	17.0
as above, with presentation finish	32.0	25.0
with tone illustrations, three or more colours	42.0	35.0
as above, with presentation finish	55.0	45.0

Notes

1. INTRODUCTION

1 The more important works are (in order of publication): H. Swayze, *Political control of literature in the USSR, 1946–1959* (Harvard, 1962); M. Friedberg, 'Soviet books, censors and readers', in M. Hayward & L. Labedz, eds., *Literature and revolution in Soviet Russia* (Oxford, 1963), pp. 198–210; M. Friedberg, 'Literary output 1956–1962', in M. Hayward & E. L. Crowley, eds., *Soviet literature in the sixties* (London, 1965), pp. 150–77; R. Conquest, ed., *The politics of ideas in the USSR* (London, 1967); P. Hübner, 'Aspekte der sowjetischen Zensur', *Osteuropa*, 1972(1), 1–24; L. Vladimirov, 'Glavlit: how the Soviet censor works', *Index*, 1972(1), 31–43; M. Dewhirst & R. Farrell, eds., *The Soviet censorship* (Metuchen, 1973); D. A. Loeber, 'Samizdat under Soviet law', in D. D. Barry et al., eds., *Contemporary Soviet law* (The Hague, 1974), pp. 84–123; F. J. M. Feldbrugge, *Samizdat and political dissent in the USSR* (Leyden, 1975); M. Dewhirst, 'Soviet Russian literature and literary policy', in A. Brown & M. Kaser, eds., *The Soviet Union since the fall of Khrushchev* (London, 1975), pp. 181–95; G. D. Hollander, 'Political communication and dissent in the Soviet Union', in R. L. Tökes, ed., *Dissent in the USSR* (Baltimore, 1975), pp. 263–8; P. B. Maggs, 'Legal controls on American publication of heterodox Soviet writings', in ibid., pp. 310–25; A. A. Yakushev, 'The samizdat movement in the USSR', *Russian review*, 34 (1975), 186–93.

2 G. D. Hollander, *Soviet political indoctrination: developments in mass media and propaganda since Stalin* (N.Y., 1972), pp. 83–98. Book publishing is not dealt with at all in the two other recent substantial treatments of the Soviet mass media: M. W. Hopkins, *Mass media in the Soviet Union* (N.Y., 1970), and I. de S. Pool, 'Communication in totalitarian societies', in I. de S. Pool, ed., *Handbook of communication* (Chicago, 1973), pp. 462–511.

3 L. I. Brezhnev, in his speech at the 24th Party Congress, enumerated as 'means of mass information and propaganda' only newspapers, journals, television, radio and information agencies: *Materialy XXIV s''ezda KPSS* (M., 1971), p. 89.

4 The most detailed reports of this kind are those of the delegations of American book publishers which visited the USSR in 1962 and 1970, issued together as *Book publishing in the USSR* (Harvard/Oxford, 1972). Shorter accounts are the reports of the delegations from the (British) Publishers' Association on their visits in 1964, 1966, 1970 and 1974, which have not been made available to the public; and D. R. Ellegood's article, 'Book publishing in the USSR', *Scholarly publishing*, 4 (1972), 81–90.

5 A history of Soviet studies in this field is V. A. Markus, 'Organizatsiya i ekonomika izdatel'skogo dela: etapy formirovaniya nauchnoi distsipliny, istochniki, nekotorye problemy', *Kniga*, 15 (1967), 191–211. The current Soviet standard works on contemporary book publishing show the same inclination: V. A. Markus, *Organizatsiya i ekonomika izdatel'skogo dela*, 3rd ed. (M., 1976); and, at a more elementary level, S. F. Dobkin, *Osnovy izdatel'skogo dela i knigopechataniya*, 2nd ed. (M., 1972).

6 Cf. R. A. Bauer & K. J. Gergen, eds., *The study of policy formation* (N.Y., 1968), p. 2.

7 Cf. Z. Brzezinski & S. P. Huntington, *Political power USA / USSR* (London, 1964), p. 6, where a similar description of the policy-making process also includes 'formulating issues for decision'.

8 The Bodleian Library, Oxford, is believed to hold the only nearly complete set of this journal in the UK, partly on microfilm and wanting only two issues.

9 E. O. Maio-Znak, in 'O sopostavimosti pokazatelei statistiki vypuska izdanii s dannymi otchetov izdatel'stv', *Izd. delo. Ref. inf.*, 1974(10), 14–19, relates that the Vysshaya Shkola publishing-house was recorded by the All-Union Book Chamber as issuing 572 books and pamphlets in 1972, while the house itself listed 1012! The usual cause of such conflicting figures is said to be disagreement over the classification of *trudy* and similar irregular series.

2. THE POLITICAL AND ECONOMIC VIEW OF SOVIET PUBLISHING

1 V. A. Markus, *Organizatsiya i ekonomika izdatel'skogo dela*, 3rd ed. (M., 1976), p. 8.

2 *Pechat' SSSR v 1975 godu*, p. 7.

3 A. S. Myl'nikov, 'Marks i Engel's o knige', *Kniga*, 7 (1962), 31–2, 63.

4 V. G. Kamyshev, *Prava avtorov literaturnykh proizvedenii* (M., 1972), pp. 42–3.

5 V. Z. Marshak, 'Finansovyi mekhanizm formirovaniya fondov material'nogo pooshchreniya v izdatel'stvakh', *Izd. delo. Ref. inf.*, 1973(5), 3.

6 I. A. Stolyarov, *Optimizatsionnye modeli planirovaniya izdatel'skoi deyatel'nosti*, dissertation summary (M., 1974), p. 6.

7 V. A. Markus, 'Organizatsiya i ekonomika izdatel'skogo dela . . .', *Kniga*, 15 (1967), 192, 198–200.

8 L. S. Glyazer, 'Ekonomiko-matematicheskaya model' izdatel'skoi deyatel'nosti', in *Optimal'noe planirovanie i sovershenstvovanie upravleniya narodnym khozyaistvom* (M., 1969), pp. 423–4.

9 V. Z. Marshak, 'Finansy izdatel'stv', *Kniga*, 22 (1971), 37–9.

10 A. A. Govorov, 'K voprosu o teorii knizhnoi torgovli', in *Vtoraya Vsesoyuznaya nauchnaya konferentsiya po problemam knigovedeniya*, 11 vols. (M., 1974), vol. 7, p. 25.

11 M. Solodkov, 'Ekonomicheskie problemy neproizvodstvennoi sfery', *Ekonomicheskie nauki*, 1974(10), 10.

12 *Metodicheskie ukazaniya k razrabotke gosudarstvennykh planov razvitiya narodnogo khozyaistva SSSR* (M., 1974), pp. 151–2, 553–4, 744, 761, 781, 784–5.

13 A. Gerasimenko, 'Akkumuliruya luchshee', *V mire knig*, 1975(12), 10–11.
14 V. Ezhkov, G. Martirosyan & M. Chetyrkin, 'Vazhnoe zveno propagandy nauchno-tekhnicheskikh dostizhenii', *Kommunist*, 1974(15), 118–19.
15 N. V. Dinamova, *Issledovanie putei povysheniya effektivnosti knizhnoi produktsii i rentabel'nosti izdatel'stv i knizhnoi torgovli*, dissertation summary (M., 1970), p. 23.
16 D. Tsmokalenko, 'Chest' i dolg izdatelya', *V mire knig*, 1975(6), 5.
17 R. G. Abdullin, 'O rabote redaktora s avtorom v knizhnom izdatel'stve', *Kniga*, 11 (1965), 111–12.
18 Glyazer (note 8), pp. 424–6.
19 B. S. Gorbachevskii, 'Opredelenie effektivnosti knigoizdatel'skoi deyatel'nosti', *Kniga*, 31 (1975), 39–40.
20 S. F. Dobkin, *Osnovy izdatel'skogo dela i knigopechataniya*, 2nd ed. (M., 1972), pp. 237–8, 247–8.
21 *Spravochnik normativnykh materialov dlya izdatel'skikh rabotnikov*, 2nd ed. (M., 1977), pp. 111–12.
22 G. A. Kovalev, *Sovershenstvovanie ucheta i analiza khozyaistvennoi deyatel'nosti v sfere kul'tury*, dissertation summary (M., 1970), pp. 13–14.
23 I. P. Korovkin, 'Sovershenstvovanie planirovaniya knigoizdatel'skoi deyatel'nosti', *Poligrafiya*, 1977(1), 10.
24 *Voprosy ideologicheskoi raboty KPSS* (M., 1972), pp. 553–4.
25 I. P. Korovkin, 'Opyt raboty izdatel'stv v novykh usloviyakh khozyaistvennoi reformy', *Izd. delo. Ref. inf.*, 1976(10), 10–11.
26 I. P. Korovkin, 'Zadanie chetvertogo goda pyatiletki – dosrochno', *Poligrafiya*, 1974(2), 2.
27 Markus (note 7), p. 193.
28 V. Astakhov, 'Khozraschet i nauchnaya kniga', *Voprosy ekonomiki*, 1966(9), 128–31.
29 V. Z. Marshak, 'Okupit' zatraty ili snizit'?', *V mire knig*, 1975(10), 22.
30 M. Maslovatyi, 'K voprosu o sisteme natural'nykh pokazatelei', *Poligrafiya*, 1974(9), 12.
31 Dinamova (note 15), pp. 8–10, 21–3.
32 Gorbachevskii (note 19), pp. 45–6.
33 As described in M. Ellman, *Planning problems in the USSR* (Cambridge, 1973), p. 124.
34 Stolyarov (note 6), pp. 9–11.
35 G. Gorbunov, 'Perspektiva i ee izmereniya', *V mire knig*, 1975(9), 6–7.
36 N. M. Sikorskii & E. L. Nemirovskii, 'Knigovedenie i ego zadachi v svete aktual'nykh problem sovetskogo knizhnogo dela', in *Vtoraya Vsesoyuznaya...* (note 10), vol. 1, pp. 9–10.
37 Percentages calculated from data in *Pechat' SSSR v 1971 godu*, pp. 4, 56, 65–6.
38 E. F. Mizhenskaya, *Lichnye potrebnosti pri sotsializme* (M., 1973), p. 127; and *Narodnoe khozyaistvo SSSR v 1975g.*, pp. 624–5.
39 A. S. Makhov, 'O nekotorykh itogakh vypuska literatury v devyatoi pyatiletki...', *Izd. delo. Ref. inf.*, 1975(6), 22.
40 Many references are given in V. P. Vasil'ev, 'Chitatel'skii interes kak problema effektivnosti pechatnoi propagandy', in *Voprosy teorii i praktiki massovykh sredstv propagandy*, issue 3 (M., 1970), pp. 219–57; I. P.

Osipova & A. I. Lebedeva, 'Sotsiologiya knigi i chteniya', in *Bibliotekovedenie v 1968–1970gg.* (M., 1971), pp. 35–62; and I. P. Osipova, 'Sotsiologiya knigi i chteniya', in *Bibliotekovedenie v 1970–1972gg.* (M., 1973), pp. 64–80.

41 'Vsesoyuznaya konferentsiya "Problemy chteniya i formirovanie cheloveka razvitogo sotsialisticheskogo obshchestva"', *Sovetskoe bibliotekovedenie*, 1973(6), 49, 56–7.

42 *Kniga i chtenie v zhizni nebol'shikh gorodov* (M., 1973).

43 In 1975 unpriced publications accounted for 3.8 per cent of copies of books and pamphlets issued in the USSR (*Pechat' SSSR v 1975 godu*, p. 9).

44 N. M. Sikorskii, *Teoriya i praktika redaktirovaniya* (M., 1971), p. 198.

3. THE COMMUNIST PARTY

1 R. H. McNeal, *Guide to the decisions of the Communist Party of the Soviet Union* (Toronto, 1972), pp. xii–xiii.

2 R. Conquest, ed., *The politics of ideas in the USSR* (London, 1967), pp. 97–9; A. Avtorkhanov, *The Communist Party apparatus* (Chicago, 1966), p. 201.

3 B. Harasymiw, 'Nomenklatura: the Soviet Communist Party's leadership recruitment system', *Canadian journal of political science*, 2 (1969), 497–8; Avtorkhanov (note 2), p. 21.

4 *Voprosy ideologicheskoi raboty KPSS* (M., 1972), pp. 554–6.

5 *O partiinoi i sovetskoi pechati, radioveshchanii i televidenii* (M., 1972), p. 458.

6 Ibid., pp. 469–71.

7 *Voprosy ideologicheskoi raboty KPSS* (M., 1972), p. 548.

8 'Vnimanie – izobrazitel'noi produktsii', *Kn. obozrenie*, 1973(27), 2.

9 *Trud i zarabotnaya plata rabotnikov izdatel'stv i redaktsii zhurnalov* (M., 1973), pp. 129–30.

10 Ibid., p. 126.

11 A section head of the Department of Propaganda reported on a review of publishers' plans at a conference of publishing administrators in early 1977 ('Khorosho podgotovit'sya k yubileyu', *Kn. obozrenie*, 1977(10), 2). On the increased importance of the Central Committee departments after the Ideological Commission's abolition in 1965, see L. G. Churchward, *The Soviet intelligentsia* (London, 1973), pp. 141–2.

12 I. A. Veselov, 'Tematicheskoe planirovanie izdaniya literatury i organizatsiya raboty...', *Izd. delo. Ref. inf.*, 1976(5), 13.

13 *Trud i zarabotnaya plata...* (note 9), pp. 124–8.

14 *Voprosy ideologicheskoi raboty KPSS*, 2nd ed. (M., 1973), p. 604–5.

15 Ibid., pp. 524–8.

16 G. D. Hollander, *Soviet political indoctrination* (N.Y., 1972), p. 48–50.

17 A. S. Makhov, 'O nekotorykh itogakh vypuska literatury v devyatoi pyatiletke...', *Izd. delo. Ref. inf.*, 1975(6), 17.

18 V. S. Moldovan, 'Izdatel'stvo "Ekonomika", vypolnit svoi zadachi', *Izd. delo. Knigovedenie. Ref. inf.*, 1971(12), 37.

19 *O partiinoi i sovetskoi pechati...* (note 5), pp. 458–9.

20 *Administrativnoe pravo* (M., 1967), p. 425n, citing *Sobranie postanov-lenii pravitel'stva SSSR*, 1966(19), para. 171.

21 L. Finkelstein, in M. Dewhirst & R. Farrell, eds., *The Soviet censorship* (Metuchen, 1973), pp. 55, 65–6.

22 'Vse sily na vypolneniya prinyatykh reshenii', *Poligrafiya*, 1974(10), 2–4.

23 *Uchreditel'nyi s"ezd Vsesoyuznogo dobrovol'nogo obshchestva lyubitelei knigi. Materialy* (M., 1975), p. 142.

24 'Ucheba rabotnikov pechati', *Kn. obozrenie*, 1975(52), 3. On such courses in general, see L. Révész, 'Die ideologisch-politische Parteischulung in der Sowjetunion', *Osteuropa*, 19 (1969), 820–1.

25 N. G. Bogdanov & B. A. Vyazemskii, *Spravochnik zhurnalista*, 3rd ed. (Leningrad, 1971), p. 47.

26 V. Khropotinskii, 'Istochnik tvorchestva – znaniya', *V mire knig*, 1975 (12), 7.

27 *O partiinoi i sovetskoi pechati* . . . (note 5), pp. 460–3.

28 O. V. Vadeev, 'Podgotovka i redaktirovanie massovo-politicheskoi literatury', *Izd. delo. Ref. inf.*, 1974(2), 18.

29 J. F. Hough, *The Soviet prefects* (Harvard, 1969), p. 16.

30 A. Dolzhenko, 'Preodolenie stereotipa', *V mire knig*, 1974(8), 7–9.

31 N. Kuznetsova, 'Lipetsskii prezent', *Sovetskaya kul'tura*, 17 June 1975, 3. For further details, see 9.8.

32 A. Zvonova, 'Rozhdennoe pyatiletkoi', *V mire knig*, 1975(8), 21.

33 A. Gerasimenko, 'Organizatsiya vnutriizdatel'skogo khozrascheta', *Kn. torgovlya*, 1971(6), 9.

34 *Partiinaya zhizn'*, 1975(8), 63.

35 *Ekonomika poligraficheskoi promyshlennosti* (M., 1972), pp. 133–4.

36 P. Luchinskii, ' "Luminitsy" sel'skikh ulits', *V mire knig*, 1974(2), 27.

37 T. A. Boiko, 'O praktike izucheniya sprosa v knigotorgovykh organi-zatsiyakh BSSR', *Izd. delo. Knigovedenie. Ref. inf.*, 1971(8), 55.

38 *O partiinoi i sovetskoi pechati* . . . (note 5), pp. 496–8.

39 *Byulleten' Ministerstva vysshego i srednego spetsial'nogo obrazovaniya SSSR*, 1975(12), 33.

40 'Otchet Tsentral'noi revizionnoi komissii KPSS', *Pravda*, 26 February 1976, 2.

41 R. H. McNeal, 'Paying for the Party', *Survey*, 1976(2), 57–68.

42 *Redaktirovanie otdel'nykh vidov literatury* (M., 1973), p. 311.

43 *Spravochnik normativnykh materialov dlya izdatel'skikh rabotnikov* (M., 1969), p. 52.

44 Ya. I. Arest & V. A. Dobrushin, *Bibliotechnye kollektory* (M., 1973), pp. 62–3.

4. THE GOVERNMENT APPARATUS

1 The session of 17 April 1975 is reported in unusual detail in *Izd. delo. Ref. inf.*, 1975(6).

2 N. G. Malykhin, *Ocherki po istorii knigoizdatel'skogo dela v SSSR* (M., 1965), pp. 384–437.

3 *Funktsii i struktura organov upravleniya* (M., 1973), pp. 90, 93.

4 Interview with staff of State Committee for Publishing, 5 March 1975.

5 *Sobranie postanovlenii pravitel'stva SSSR*, 1973(23), 547–58.
6 V. A. Markus, *Organizatsiya i ekonomika izdatel'skogo dela*, 3rd ed. (M., 1976), p. 28.
7 Report in *Kn. obozrenie*, 1975(11), 2.
8 'Tovarishch kniga', *Literaturnaya gazeta*, 2 June 1976, 3.
9 *Prominent personalities in the USSR* (Metuchen, 1968), p. 610.
10 News item in *V mire knig*, 1973(11), 67.
11 'Memuary – letopis' epokhi', *V mire knig*, 1975(12), 46.
12 Interview with Deputy Chief Editor for Scientific and Technical Literature, 6 March 1975.
13 V. Chalidze, *To defend these rights* (London, 1975), p. 81.
14 V. Ezhkov, G. Martirosyan & M. Chetyrkin, 'Vazhnoe zveno propagandy nauchno-tekhnicheskikh dostizhenii', *Kommunist*, 1974(15), 120–1.
15 *Ekonomika poligraficheskoi promyshlennosti* (M., 1972), pp. 244–5.
16 I. Korovkin, 'Nekotorye voprosy povysheniya ekonomicheskoi effektivnosti knigoizdatel'skogo dela', *Poligrafiya*, 1975(2), 6–8.
17 B. A. Korchagin, *Material'no-tekhnicheskoe snabzhenie v poligrafii* (M., 1972), pp. 10–12, 19, 24, 76–92.
18 'V Goskomizdate SSSR', *V mire knig*, 1973(11), 25.
19 'Gorizonty "Kazakhstana" ', *Kn. obozrenie*, 1975(7), 2.
20 'Opyt knigoizdaniya v soyuznykh respublikakh', *Izd. delo. Ref. inf.*, 1975(6), 56.
21 A. Khanbabaev, 'Tsel' i inertsiya', *V mire knig*, 1974(7), 7.
22 *Normativnye materialy po izdatel'skomu delu dlya organizatsii ministerstv i vedomstv* (M., 1973), p. 11.
23 *Voprosy ideologicheskoi raboty KPSS* (M., 1972), p. 558.
24 E. N. Rapinya, 'Nekotorye voprosy uluchsheniya knigoizdatel'skoi deyatel'nosti v Latviiskoi SSR', *Izd. delo. Knigovedenie. Ref. inf.*, 1972(6), 37.
25 'Distsiplina dlya vsekh odna', *V mire knig*, 1973(10), 21.
26 *Trud i zarabotnaya plata rabotnikov izdatel'stv i redaktsii zhurnalov* (M., 1973), p. 307.
27 *Spravochnik normativnykh materialov dlya izdatel'skikh rabotnikov*, 2nd ed. (M., 1977), p. 14. The earlier regulations are on pp. 9–13 of the previous edition (M., 1969).
28 V. G. Kamyshev, *Prava avtorov literaturnykh proizvedenii* (M., 1972), pp. 135, 158.
29 A. A. Nebenzya, 'Ne nadstroika – sostavnaya chast'', *V mire knig*, 1976 (12), 7–8.
30 Korovkin (note 16), p. 7.
31 Nebenzya (note 29), p. 6.
32 A. A. Nebenzya, 'O sostoyanii i zadachakh po dal'neishemu sovershenstvovaniyu svodnogo tematicheskogo planirovaniya . . .', *Izd. delo. Ref. inf.*, 1976(12), 16.
33 *Metodicheskie ukazaniya k razrabotke gosudarstvennykh planov razvitiya narodnogo khozyaistva SSSR* (M., 1974), pp. 151–2, 553–4.
34 V. Z. Marshak, 'Izdatel'stvo – tipografiya', *Poligrafiya*, 1974(1), 21–2.
35 L. M. Konshina, 'Sovershenstvovanie planirovaniya deyatel'nosti izdatel'stv . . .', *Izd. delo. Knigovedenie. Ref. inf.*, 1972(6), 5–10.

36 I. Korovkin, 'O vnedrenii avtomatizirovannykh sistem upravleniya v knigoizdatel'skom dele', *Poligrafiya*, 1975(8), 6.
37 N. A. Shibik, 'Nekotorye voprosy optimizatsii izdatel'skogo dela v usloviyakh novoi sistemy khozyaistvovaniya', *Izd. delo. Ref. inf.*, 1974 (4), 4.
38 I. P. Korovkin, 'Analiz i perspektiva', *V mire knig*, 1976(4), 7.
39 *Izd. delo. Ref. inf.*, 1976(8) is devoted entirely to an account of this process.
40 I. P. Korovkin, 'O vnedrenii avtomatizirovannykh sistem upravleniya v knigoizdatel'skoe delo', *Izd. delo. Ref. inf.*, 1975(6), 42.
41 B. Alekseev, 'ASU–PECHAT'–TORG', *V mire knig*, 1976(3), 41–3.
42 S. S. Panterov, 'O sozdanii avtomatizirovannoi sistemy podgotovki i vypuska izdanii gosudarstvennoi bibliografii vo Vsesoyuznoi knizhnoi palate', *Sovetskaya bibliografiya*, 1974(5), 3–8.

5. THE PUBLISHING-HOUSE

1 *Funktsii i struktura organov upravleniya* (M., 1973), p. 245.
2 V. A. Markus, 'Khozraschet v izdatel'stve v svete poslednikh reshenii partii', *Kniga*, 14 (1967), 11–12.
3 *Spravochnik normativnykh materialov dlya izdatel'skikh rabotnikov* (M., 1969), pp. 14–30.
4 A. Gerasimenko, 'Organizatsiya vnutriizdatel'skogo khozrascheta', *Kn. torgovlya*, 1971(6), 9–10.
5 A. E. Mil'chin, *Metodika i tekhnika redaktirovaniya teksta* (M., 1972), pp. 6–7, 14–15. The requirement that the names of editors and proof-readers should be stated in every book originates in a letter from Lenin to the State Publishing-House of 11 December 1920, which saw the measure as a means of establishing individual responsibility for any errors in a work (Lenin, *Sobranie sochinenii*, 5th ed., vol. 52 (M., 1965), pp. 28–9).
6 *Trud i zarabotnaya plata rabotnikov izdatel'stv i redaktsii zhurnalov* (M., 1973), p. 78.
7 R. G. Abdullin, 'Tematicheskii plan i redaktor', *Kniga*, 17 (1968), 77.
8 Interview with chief editor of Mysl', 31 July 1973.
9 Abdullin (note 7), p. 91.
10 L. A. Konikov, 'O nekotorykh aspektakh raboty izdatel'skogo redaktora', *Izd. delo. Ref. inf.*, 1974(6), 14.
11 B. I. Stukalin, 'Osnovnye zadachi izdatel'stv po vypusku obshchestvenno-politicheskoi literatury v svete trebovanii XXIV s"ezda KPSS', *Izd. delo. Knigovedenie. Ref. inf.*, 1971(12), 9.
12 *Spravochnik . . .* (note 3), p. 92.
13 V. Ezhkov, G. Martirosyan & M. Chetyrkin, 'Vazhnoe zveno propagandy nauchno-tekhnicheskikh dostizhenii', *Kommunist*, 1974(15), 120.
14 F. S. Veinberg, 'Obshchestvennye nachala v rabote Politizdata', *Izd. delo. Knigovedenie. Ref. inf.*, 1972(5), 13–14.
15 V. V. Musakov, 'Opyt organizatsii vnutriizdatel'skogo khozrascheta', *Izd. delo. Knigovedenie. Ref. inf.*, 1971(3), 4.
16 I. Korovkin, 'Khozyaistvennyi raschet i potentsial proizvodstva', *V mire knig*, 1974(4), 5–6.

17 Authors' fees were paid for only 43 per cent of books (measured in author's sheets) in the Ukrainian SSR in 1970 (*Vtoraya Vsesoyuznaya nauchnaya konferentsiya po problemam knigovedeniya*, 11 vols. (M., 1974), vol. 6, p. 13).

18 I. P. Korovkin, 'Planirovanie i ekonomicheskoe stimulirovanie v knigoizdatel'skom dele', *Izd. delo. Ref. inf.*, 1974(5), 6–7.

19 I. P. Korovkin, 'Izdatel'stva v novykh usloviyakh', *Ekonomicheskaya gazeta*, 1969(5), 15.

20 Abdullin (note 7), p. 83–4.

21 P. V. Grechishnikov, 'Opyt primeneniya novoi sistemy planirovaniya i ekonomicheskogo stimulirovaniya', *Izd. delo. Ref. inf.*, 1974(5), 8.

22 *Spravochnik normativnykh materialov dlya rabotnikov knizhnoi torgovli* (M., 1970), p. 15.

23 V. G. Kamyshev, *Prava avtorov literaturnykh proizvedenii* (M., 1972), p. 107.

24 B. Kuropatkin, 'Srodni ogranshchiku', *V mire knig*, 1977(2), 4.

25 V. G. Yuzbashev, 'Obshchestvennye redaktsii izdatel'stva "Yuridicheskaya literatura" ', *Izd. delo. Knigovedenie. Ref. inf.*, 1972(5), 35–6.

26 *Spravochnik*. . . (note 3), p. 92.

27 'Tipovoi izdatel'skii dogovor na literaturnye proizvedeniya', *Byuleten' normativnykh aktov ministerstv i vedomstv SSSR*, 1975(7), 35.

28 Kamyshev (note 23), p. 32.

29 V. L. Chertkov, *Sudebnaya zashchita prav i interesov avtorov* (M., 1971), p. 61.

30 *Sobranie dokumentov samizdata*, vol. 20, AS no. 1002, pp. 5–9.

31 A. M. Garibyan, *Avtorskoe pravo na proizvedeniya nauki* (Erevan, 1974), pp. 176–7.

32 'Tipovoi izdatel'skii dogovor . . .' (note 27), p. 35.

33 V. A. Markus, 'O nekotorykh novykh normativnykh dokumentakh v knigoizdatel'skom dele', *Kniga*, 18 (1969), 53.

34 *Spravochnik*. . . (note 3), p. 104.

35 Ibid., p. 26.

36 L. S. Drozdova, 'Povyshenie effektivnosti sistemy oplaty truda i normirovaniya raboty v izdatel'stvakh', *Izd. delo. Ref. inf.*, 1976(10), 23–4. The full scales were not available to me at the time of writing.

37 *Trud i zarabotnaya plata*. . . (note 6), pp. 140–6.

38 Interview with director of Russkii Yazyk publishing-house, 18 March 1975.

39 *Trud i zarabotnaya plata*. . . (note 6), pp. 302–17.

40 V. A. Markus, *Organizatsiya i ekonomika izdatel'skogo dela*, 3rd ed, (M., 1976), p. 201.

41 *Trud i zarabotnaya plata*. . . (note 6), pp. 164–97.

42 P. Grechishnikov, 'Effektivnost', glasnost', sostyazatel'nost'', *V mire knig*, 1973(9), 4.

43 Korovkin (note 18), p. 6.

44 Interview with Deputy Chief Editor for Scientific and Technical Literature, State Committee for Publishing, 6 March 1975.

45 I. P. Korovkin, 'Opyt raboty izdatel'stv v novykh usloviyakh khozyaistvennoi reformy', *Izd. delo. Ref. inf.*, 1976(10), 11–12.

46 Ibid.

47 *Trud i zarabotnaya plata . . .* (note 6), pp. 92–4.

48 A work is said to be in the house's 'contract portfolio' from the signature of a contract with the author to the point at which the manuscript receives the house's approval (*odobrenie*). It is then transferred to the 'editorial portfolio', and subsequently, on reaching the production department, to the 'production portfolio'.

49 Interviews with directors of Mir and Prosveshchenie, 14 March 1975 and 17 March 1975.

50 *Sostoyanie i perspektivy izucheniya sprosa na knizhnuyu produktsiyu* (M., 1974), p. 53n.

51 V. Sergeeva, 'Trudnosti "Azerkitaba" ', *V mire knig*, 1976(11), 47.

52 *Spravochnik . . .* (note 3), p. 20.

53 Interview with deputy head of Glavkniga, 11 March 1975.

54 N. I. Bychkova, 'Formy i metody propagandy i reklamy izdanii', *Izd. delo. Ref. inf.*, 1973(9), 11–12.

55 Interview with deputy head of Glavkniga, 11 March 1975.

56 M. Dewhirst & R. Farrell, eds., *The Soviet censorship* (Metuchen, 1973), p. 63n.

57 I owe this note on the absence of censorship numbers in foreign fiction to Mr A. H. Brown.

58 Translated in B. I. Gorokhoff, *Publishing in the USSR* (Bloomington, 1959), pp. 258–60, and in R. Conquest, ed., *The politics of ideas in the USSR* (London, 1967), pp. 61–3. Both state the Russian original to be in *Ugolovnyi kodeks RSFSR* (M., 1957), pp. 143–5. It is not printed in the 1970 edition of that code. *Encyclopedia of Soviet law* (Leiden, 1973), p. 600, states that it was renewed in an (unspecified) decree of 15 September 1966.

59 Dewhirst & Farrell (note 56), p. 51, and personal observation in two Moscow publishing-houses, March 1975.

60 G. E. Gryunberg, 'Uporyadochenie vedomstvennoi izdatel'skoi deyatel'nosti v Estonii', *Izd. delo. Ref. inf.*, 1973(12), 9.

61 *Normativnye materialy po izdatel'skomu delu dlya organizatsii ministerstv i vedomstv* (M., 1973), pp. 62–6.

62 Dewhirst & Farrell (note 56), p. 58.

63 Z. A. Medvedev, *Ten years after Ivan Denisovich* (Harmondsworth, 1975), p. 70.

64 'Glavlit', *Posev*, 1968(7), 52. The article appears from internal evidence to have been written by L. Finkelstein (pseudonym L. Vladimirov).

65 'USSR: political errors', *Index on censorship*, 1976(2), 77.

66 Dewhirst & Farrell (note 56), pp. 2, 73–4, 83, 86–8.

6. THE AUTHOR

1 *Osnovy grazhdanskogo zakonodatel'stva* (M., 1962), referred to below as *OGZ*. Amendments consequent upon the Soviet Union's adherence to the Universal Copyright Convention are made in *Vedomosti Verkhovnogo Soveta SSSR*, 1973(9), 131–2.

2 E.g. *Grazhdanskii kodeks RSFSR*, articles 475–516, referred to below as

GK RSFSR. The 1976 edition incorporates amendments consequent upon adherence to the Universal Copyright Convention, originally made in *Vedomosti Verkhovnogo Soveta RSFSR*, 1974(10), 163–8.

3 *GK RSFSR*, art. 5.

4 In Russian, *opublikovanie, vosproizvedenie i rasprostranenie. Opubliko-vanie* can apply to the presentation of a play, exhibition of a picture, or to making a work available by special permission, as well as to the publication of a book. This latter English phrase covers two Russian expressions, *izdanie* and *vypusk v svet*, the second of which carries the added sense of making the work publicly accessible. See *Nauchno-prakticheskii kommentarii k GK RSFSR* (M., 1966), pp. 547–8, and D. A. Loeber, 'Samizdat under Soviet law', in D. D. Barry et al., eds., *Contemporary Soviet law* (The Hague, 1974), pp. 100–1n. A work circu-lated 'as manuscript' (*na pravakh rukopisi*) to an unrestricted public would still be regarded as *vypushchennoe v svet*, but *GK RSFSR*, art. 476, does allow reproduction 'as manuscript' for a restricted group of recipients in certain circumstances without ranking as *vypusk v svet*. It has been suggested that the formula *na pravakh rukopisi* is often used by the author to disarm criticism and evade full responsibility for the work (A. Perttsik, 'Na pravakh rukopisi', *Sovetskoe gosudarstvo i pravo*, 1951 (1), 57–8).

5 *OGZ*, art. 98; *GK RSFSR*, art. 479.

6 *Nauchno-prakticheskii kommentarii k GK RSFSR* (M., 1966), p. 550, citing *GK RSFSR*, art. 10 in support; but this article of the code simply allows the citizen author's rights in works of science, literature, etc., without specific restriction.

7 V. G. Kamyshev, *Prava avtorov literaturnykh proizvedenii* (M., 1972), pp. 12–14.

8 *GK RSFSR*, art. 502.

9 *OGZ*, arts. 103–4, and *GK RSFSR*, arts. 492–5, all as amended.

10 'Tipovoi izdatel'skii dogovor na literaturnye proizvedeniya', *Byulleten' normativnykh aktov ministerstv i vedomstv SSSR*, 1975(7), 34–7.

11 A. E. Mil'chin, 'Vazhnaya zadacha redaktorskogo analiza', *Izd. delo. Ref. inf.*, 1974(7), 9–10.

12 M. Voronkova, 'Tipovye avtorskie dogovory', *Sovetskaya yustitsiya*, 1975(22), 6.

13 V. Kharuto, 'Rassmotrenie sudami sporov ob avtorskom voznagrazhdenii za proizvedeniya nauki, literatury i iskusstva', *Sovetskaya yustitsiya*, 1975(14), 5.

14 M. A. Lebedeva, 'Opyt redaktirovaniya "Filosofskoi biblioteki dlya yunoshestva" ', *Izd. delo. Ref. inf.*, 1974(2), 25.

15 Eight sheets at the scale for popular scientific literature in force at the time of publication (100–300r. per sheet), plus 50 per cent for an edition size between 100 000 and 200 000 copies.

16 *Spravochnik normativnykh materialov dlya izdatel'skikh rabotnikov*, 2nd ed. (M., 1977), p. 358.

17 A. M. Garibyan, *Avtorskoe pravo na proizvedeniya nauki* (Erevan, 1975), p. 112.

18 V. Marshak, 'Gonorar? Net, voznagrazhdenie', *V mire knig*, 1975(11), 23.

19 V. A. Markus, *Organizatsiya i ekonomika izdatel'skogo dela*, 3rd ed. (M., 1976), p. 252.

20 *Spravochnik po nalogam i sboram s naseleniya* (M., 1973), p. 39.

21 M. L. Platova, 'O nekotorykh problemakh khozyaistvenno-ekonomiches-koi deyatel'nosti respublikanskikh izdatel'stv', *Izd. delo. Knigovedenie. Ref. inf.*, 1970(5), 14.

22 I. P. Korovkin, 'Povyshenie rentabel'nosti izdatel'skoi deyatel'nosti v usloviyakh ekonomicheskoi reformy', *Izd. delo. Ref. inf.*, 1975(2), 10–11.

23 Citations in H. Swayze, *Political control of literature in the USSR 1946–1959* (Harvard, 1962), p. 244.

24 L. Soslovskii, 'Pust' gonorar podozhdet', *Literaturnaya gazeta*, 29 October 1975, 13.

25 *OGZ*, art. 102, and *GK RSFSR*, art. 491, both as amended.

26 'O stavkakh avtorskogo voznagrazhdeniya za izdanie proizvedenii nauki, literatury i iskusstva', *Sobranie postanovlenii pravitel'stva RSFSR*, 1975(9), 151–2, 172–4.

27 'Vo Vsesoyuznom agentstve po avtorskim pravam', *Izvestiya*, 27 December 1973, 2; and N. S. Roudakov & I. A. Gringolts, 'L'agence de l'URSS pour les droits d'auteur (VAAP)', *Revue internationale du droit d'auteur*, 81 (July 1974), 2–33.

28 V. Kharuto, 'Avtor imeet pravo . . .', *Zhurnalist*, 1975(3), 62–3. VAAP's main predecessor, VUOAP, dealt with 1463 disputes between 1967 and 1970, including 214 court cases, of which 204 were decided in the author's favour (*Pyatyi s''ezd pisatelei SSSR* (M., 1972), pp. 201–2).

29 M. M. Boguslavskii & E. P. Gavrilov, 'Avtorskoe pravo: izmeneniya i dal'neishee razvitie', *Sovetskoe gosudarstvo i pravo*, 1975(6), 22–3. The writers argue that, since the parties to an author's contract are the author or his assign on the one hand and an organisation on the other, only a corporate body, *not* an individual citizen, may be granted rights by an author.

30 *Byulleten' normativnykh aktov ministerstv i vedomstv SSSR*, 1975(7), 42–4.

31 'Prava avtora, prava izdatelya', *Literaturnaya gazeta*, 19 June 1974, 2.

32 'O vnesenii izmenenii i dopolnenii v Postanovlenie Plenuma Verkhovnogo Suda SSSR ot 19 dekabrya 1967g. No. 9', *Byulleten' Verkhovnogo Suda SSSR*, 1975(2), 22.

33 *Ugolovnyi kodeks RSFSR* (M., 1970), arts. 70, 190–1.

34 'O podkhodnom naloge s summ, vyplachivaemykh za izdanie, ispolnenie ili inoe ispol'zovanie proizvedenii nauki, literatury i iskusstva', *Vedomosti Verkhovnogo Soveta SSSR*, 1973(37), 587–90.

35 D. M. Sutulov, *Avtorskoe pravo*, 3rd ed. (M., 1974), p. 11.

36 A. S. Makhov, 'O nekotorykh itogakh vypuska literatury v devyatoi pyatiletke . . .', *Izd. delo. Ref. inf.*, 1975(6), 15–16.

37 *Narodnoe obrazovanie, nauka i kul'tura v SSSR* (M., 1971), p. 341.

38 The most comprehensive work on the Writers' Union in recent years is J. Murray, 'The Union of Soviet Writers', unpublished PhD thesis, University of Birmingham, 1973.

39 N. G. Bogdanov & B. A. Vyazemskii, *Spravochnik zhurnalista*, 3rd ed. (M., 1971), p. 126.

40 *Tvorcheskie soyuzy v SSSR* (M., 1970), p. 32n.
41 G. Priede, 'Istina dorozhe', *V mire knig*, 1974(6), 16.
42 'Razmyshleniya o planovom ubytke', *V mire knig*, 1974(1), 24.
43 The decision on whether to publish Solzhenitsyn's *Cancer ward* in *Novyi mir* is said to have been referred by the Writers' Union to the Central Committee Secretariat and possibly even to the Politburo, but was then referred back to the Union by the Party authorities (Z. A. Medvedev, *Ten years after Ivan Denisovich* (Harmondsworth, 1975), pp. 94–6). See also Murray (note 38), pp. 171–2, 340–66.
44 D. A. Granin & D. T. Khrenkov, 'Pisatel' i izdatel'', *Literaturnaya gazeta*, 10 July 1974, 4.
45 *Spravochnik normativnykh materialov dlya izdatel'skikh rabotnikov* (M., 1969), p. 177. Murray (note 38), p. 66, through a misunderstanding of his source (*Izvestiya*, 2 December 1959, 3) erroneously states that Litfond receives 10 per cent of publishers' *receipts* on books. E. Simmons, in H. G. Skilling & F. Griffiths, eds., *Interest groups in Soviet politics* (Princeton, 1973), p. 258, states that part of the Writers' Union income comes from 6 per cent of publishing-houses' net returns. I can find no substantiation of this in Soviet sources.
46 *Pyatyi s"ezd pisatelei SSSR* (note 28), pp. 199–200.

7. PRINTING, PAPER AND SUPPLIES

1 M. Ya. Shpital'nyi, *Organizatsiya khozyaistvennogo rascheta na poligraficheskikh predpriyatiyakh* (M., 1973), pp. 5–6.
2 M. L. Platova, 'Nekotorye voprosy soglasovannoi deyatel'nosti izdatel'stv i poligraficheskikh predpriyatii', *Izd. delo. Knigovedenie. Ref. inf.*, 1971 (10), 4.
3 Interview with staff of State Committee for Publishing, 5 March 1975.
4 *Ekonomika poligraficheskoi promyshlennosti* (M., 1972), p. 34.
5 Some examples of the Inspectorate's work are given in 'Kursom sovershenstvovaniya', *Kn. obozrenie*, 1976(45), 2.
6 N. G. Miusskii, 'Nereshennye problemy sovmestnoi deyatel'nosti izdatel'stv i poligraficheskikh predpriyatii Belorussii', *Izd. delo. Knigovedenie. Ref. inf.*, 1972(6), 35.
7 I. Korovkin, 'Sovershenstvovanie planirovaniya knigoizdatel'skoi deyatel'nosti', *Poligrafiya*, 1977(1), 9.
8 *Normativnye materialy po izdatel'skomu delu dlya organizatsii ministerstv i vedomstv* (M., 1973), pp. 99–138.
9 V. N. Sinyukhin, 'Ekonomicheskaya storona vzaimootnoshenii izdatel'stv i predpriyatii poligraficheskoi promyshlennosti', *Izd. delo. Ref. inf.*, 1973(5), 6–7.
10 V. Dinkevich, 'K voprosu o vzaimootnosheniyakh izdatel'stv s poligraficheskimi predpriyatiyami', *Poligrafiya*, 1975(10), 15.
11 D. D. Zuev, 'Metody koordinatsii raboty izdatelei i poligrafistov', *Izd. delo. Knigovedenie. Ref. inf.*, 1972(6), 49.
12 F. S. Savitskii, 'Opyt koordinatsii raboty izdatel'stv i poligraficheskikh predpriyatii v Ukrainskoi SSR', *Izd. delo. Knigovedenie. Ref. inf.*, 1972 (6), 33.

13 V. N. Sinyukhin, 'Nekotorye voprosy sovershenstvovaniya otnoshenii izdatel'stv i tipografii', *Poligrafiya*, 1973(4), 9.
14 B. A. Korchagin, *Material'no-tekhnicheskoe snabzhenie v poligrafii, izdatel'skom dele, knizhnoi torgovle* (M., 1972), pp. 196–200.
15 Ibid., pp. 10–13, 162–5. The 3 per cent addition superseded an earlier figure of 5 per cent in 1977 (*Poligrafiya*, 1976(9), 5–6).
16 B. A. Korchagin, Rabota kontor material'no-tekhnicheskogo snabzheniya v novykh usloviyakh', *Poligrafiya*, 1974(6), 8–11.
17 Korchagin (note 14), pp. 76–7.
18 G. A. Gurevich, 'Nekotorye nasushchnye voprosy organizatsii i planirovaniya raboty izdatel'stv', *Izd. delo. Knigovedenie. Ref. inf.*, 1970(6), 15.
19 E. A. Dinershtein, L. A. Belaya & F. S. Sonkina, *Sovremennaya praktika pereizdaniya literatury v SSSR* (M., 1972), p. 10n.
20 T. S. Gunich, 'Ob otsenke urovnya prodazhi knig na dushu naseleniya', *Kn. torgovlya. Ref. inf.*, 1973(3), 2.
21 'Vazhnye zadachi knigoizdatelei', *Kn. obozrenie*, 1975(17), 2.
22 I. Korovkin, 'Nekotorye voprosy povysheniya ekonomicheskoi effektivnosti knigoizdatel'skogo dela', *Poligrafiya*, 1975(2), 7.
23 B. I. Stukalin, 'Sostoyanie i perspektivy vypuska literatury izdatel'stvami SSSR', *Izd. delo. Ref. inf.*, 1975(6), 10.
24 'Opyt knigoizdaniya v soyuznykh respublikakh', *Izd. delo. Ref. inf.*, 1975(6), 49.
25 L. S. Kharlampiev, 'Problemy prognozirovaniya pechati v SSSR', in *Materialy pervoi Vsesoyuznoi konferentsii po problemam knigovedeniya* (M., 1971), p. 83.
26 'Itogi razvitiya knigoizdatel'skogo dela v devyatoi pyatiletke', *Izd. delo. Ref. inf.*, 1976(2), 5.
27 *Spravochnik normativnykh materialov dlya izdatel'skikh rabotnikov* (M., 1969), pp. 231–52.
28 Zuev (note 11), pp. 48–9.
29 'V Komitete po pechati SM SSSR', *Izd. delo. Knigovedenie. Ref. inf.*, 1970(1), 51.
30 *Trud i zarabotnaya plata rabotnikov izdatel'stv i redaktsii zhurnalov* (M., 1973), p. 229.
31 'V Goskomizdate SSSR', *V mire knig*, 1975(9), 4–5.
32 Instances reported in *Literaturnaya gazeta*, 25 August 1976, 13.

8. THE BOOK TRADE

1 A. P. Marin, 'Daty, tsifry, fakty', *Kn. torgovlya. Issled. i mat.*, vol. 3 (M., 1976), p. 232. It is not made clear whether the turnover figures relate to book sales only or include other goods sold by bookshops, such as stationery.
2 B. M. Tsar'kov & G. G. Shaidurov, *Organizatsiya i tekhnologiya optovoi knizhnoi torgovli* (M., 1972), p. 6.
3 G. G. Shaidurov & A. S. Dribinskii, 'Knigotorg i izdatel'stvo', *Kn. torgovlya. Ref. inf.*, 1973(4), 8.
4 T. S. Gunich, *Ekonomicheskoe stimulirovanie v knizhnoi torgovle* (M., 1974), pp. 20–1.

5 Ibid., pp. 6, 91.
6 R. G. Abdullin, 'Tematicheskii plan i redaktor', *Kniga*, 17 (1968), 87.
7 B. Burov, 'Koordinatsiyu – na nauchnuyu osnovu', *Kn. torgovlya*, 1972 (4), 19.
8 Gunich (note 4), pp, 61, 95.
9 *Bukhgalterskii uchet i kontrol' v knizhnoi torgovle* (M., 1974), p. 10.
10 L. Ya. Rabin & A. N. Lyubimov, *Ekonomika i planirovanie torgovli knigami* (M., 1968), pp. 131–2.
11 Tsar'kov & Shaidurov (note 2), pp. 8, 49–50.
12 'Parametry rabochego rezhima', *V mire knig*, 1976(6), 27.
13 I. M. Roikhel' & E. I. Fel'dman, 'Daty, fakty, tsifry', *Kn. torgovlya. Issled. i mat.*, vol. 2 (M., 1975), pp. 211–18; and calculations from figures in I. P. Korovkin, 'Analiz i perspektiva', *V mire knig*, 1976(4), 8.
14 Tsar'kov & Shaidurov (note 2), p. 50.
15 A. P. Marin, 'Sel'skaya knizhnaya torgovlya v sisteme sovetskogo knigorasprostraneniya', *Kn. torgovlya. Issled. i mat.*, vol. 1 (M., 1974), pp. 37–8.
16 E. Ivanova, 'Pochemu ubytochen raikoopknigotorg?', *Kn. torgovlya*, 1971(3), 21.
17 M. F. Arbuzov, *Knizhnaya torgovlya v SSSR* (M., 1976), pp. 56–7.
18 N. A. Druzhininskii, 'Propaganda i reklama knigi v Leningradskom knigotorgovom ob''edinenii "Lenkniga" ', *Kn. torgovlya. Ref. inf.*, 1975 (9), 17.
19 'Problemy, postavlennye zhizn'yu', *V mire knig*, 1974(6), 43.
20 *Nauka i Tekhnika. Plan vypuska literatury 1974*, p. 3.
21 'Parametry rabochego rezhima' (note 12), p. 28.
22 V. Abolin, 'Avtoritet predvaritel'nogo zakaza', *V mire knig*, 1974(10), 42.
23 A. Kostakov, 'Knizhnyi rynok strany', *V mire knig*, 1973(11), 28.
24 *Spravochnik normativnykh materialov dlya rabotnikov knizhnoi torgovli* (M., 1970), p. 270.
25 N. M. Sikorskii & E. L. Nemirovskii, 'Knigovedenie i ee zadachi v svete aktual'nykh problem sovetskogo knizhnogo dela', in *Vtoraya Vsesoyuznaya nauchnaya konferentsiya po problemam knigovedeniya*, 11 vols. (M., 1974), vol. 1, p. 8.
26 Interview with director of Mir, 14 March 1975.
27 V. G. Utkov, *Chto nuzhno znat' kazhdomu o knizhnoi torgovle* (M., 1976), p. 27.
28 B. V. Alekseev, 'Nekotorye zadachi knizhnoi torgovli na sovremennom etape', *Kn. torgovlya. Issled. i mat.*, vol. 3 (M., 1976), p. 6.
29 *Spravochnik . . .* (note 24), pp. 28–31.
30 T. Gunich, 'Povyshat' rol' khozyaistvennykh dogovorov', *Kn. torgovlya*, 1972(3), 20–1.
31 *Spravochnik . . .* (note 24), pp. 301–4.
32 I have found no substantiation of the statement, made in the report of the American publishers' delegation to the USSR in 1970, that *authors*, as well as publishers, bear part of the loss incurred by unsold copies (*Book publishing in the USSR* (Harvard/Oxford, 1972), p. 11).
33 *Spravochnik . . .* (note 24), pp. 305–34.

34 A. Rubinov, 'Tselkovyi za makulaturu', *Literaturnaya gazeta*, 21 August 1974, 10.

35 'Knigi bez chitatelei', *Literaturnaya gazeta*, 28 August 1974, 10.

36 V. Statso, 'Po sledam "mertvykh" knig', *V mire knig*, 1973(9), 5.

37 Interview with deputy head of Glavkniga, 11 March 1975.

38 N. Marokov, 'Na bol'shoi proverke', *V mire knig*, 1976(8), 45, and correction in *V mire knig*, 1976(10), 12.

39 A. P. Marin, 'Knizhnaya torgovlya i perspektivy ee razvitiya', *Kn. torgovlya. Ref. inf.*, 1973(3), 7.

40 Marin (note 15), pp. 27–8.

41 I. Raikhman, 'Rural booklover wronged', from *Sel'skaya zhizn'*, 28 March 1974, 3, abstracted in *Current digest of the Soviet press*, 1974 (30), 21.

42 A. P. Marin, 'Progressivnye formy knigorasprostraneniya', *Kn. torgovlya. Issled. i mat.*, vol. 2 (M., 1975), p. 37.

43 Interview with deputy head of Glavkniga, 11 March 1975.

44 'The Three Musketeers from the gateway', from *Komsomolskaya pravda*, 4 November 1976, 2, translated in *Current digest of the Soviet press*, 1976(45), 7–8.

45 B. I. Stukalin, 'Magistrali knizhnoi pyatiletki', *V mire knig*, 1976(2), 3.

46 Interview with director of Mir, 14 March 1975.

47 *Trud i zarabotnaya plata rabotnikov izdatel'stv i redaktsii zhurnalov* (M., 1973), pp. 198–205.

48 'Novyi glavk Goskomizdata SSSR', *Kn. obozrenie*, 1977(24), 5.

49 *Vneshnyaya torgovlya SSSR za 1974 god*, p. 37.

50 B. K. Makarov & N. V. Gerasimov, 'Mezhdunarodnye svyazi sovetskoi knizhnoi torgovli', *Kn. torgovlya. Issled. i mat.*, vol. 1 (M., 1974), pp. 52–8. The high position of France as an importer of Soviet books is probably due to the Paris firm Les Livres Étrangers SA, which supplies Soviet publications to libraries and individuals in many Western countries.

9. SPECIAL KINDS OF PUBLICATION

1 A. S. Makhov, 'O nekotorykh itogakh vypuska literatury v devyatoi pyatiletke . . .', *Izd. delo. Ref. inf.*, 1975(6), 27–8.

2 A. A. Nebenzya, 'O sostoyanii i zadachakh po dal'neishemu sovershen-stvovaniyu svodnogo tematicheskogo planirovaniya', *Izd. delo. Ref. inf.*, 1976(12), 5.

3 I. I. Chkhikvishvili, reported in *Kn. obozrenie*, 1976(26), 4.

4 *Spravochnik normativnykh materialov dlya izdatel'skikh rabotnikov* (M., 1969), pp. 50, 52.

5 A survey of 1000 families in the Ukrainian SSR in 1967 found that an average of 42.9 per cent of books owned by each family consisted of fiction and children's books. The next largest percentage was 26.4 for school and other textbooks, followed by social and political literature with 7.6 per cent (L. P. Tikhonova, 'Nekotorye faktory, vliyayushchie na formirovanie sprosa sel'skogo naseleniya na knigi', *Izd. delo. Knigove-denie. Ref. inf.*, 1969(1), 45–7).

6 *Pechat' SSSR v 1975 godu*, pp. 23, 25.

7 'Opyt knigoizdaniya v soyuznykh respublikakh', *Izd. delo. Ref. inf.*, 1975(6), 48.

8 'Chetyre tysyachi novinok', *V mire knig*, 1974(2), 11.

9 Makhov (note 1), p. 22.

10 E. A. Dinershtein, L. A. Belaya & F. S. Sonkina, *Sovremennaya praktika pereizdaniya literatury v SSSR* (M., 1972), pp. 25–8, 42–3.

11 Nebenzya (note 2), p. 9.

12 *Voprosy ideologicheskoi raboty KPSS*, 2nd ed. (M., 1973), pp. 585–9.

13 Yu. S. Melent'ev, 'Za boevitost' i populyarnost' massovoi literatury', *Izd. delo. Ref. inf.*, 1974(2), 5–6.

14 *Rabochii – chitatel' obshchestvenno-politicheskoi literatury* (M., 1973), p. 42.

15 V. M. Vodolagin, 'Uluchshat' kachestvo izdanii', *Izd. delo. Ref. inf.*, 1974(2), 12.

16 'Usilit' propagandu politicheskoi knigi', *V mire knig*, 1975(11), 46.

17 V. A. Markus, *Organizatsiya i ekonomika izdatel'skogo dela*, 3rd ed. (M., 1976), p. 368.

18 N. V. Tropkin, 'O nekotorykh voprosakh izdaniya politicheskoi literatury', *Kniga*, 12 (1966), 8.

19 Makhov (note 1), pp. 22, 24.

20 M. F. Shpikalov, 'Knizhnyi rynok i vzaimootnosheniya izdatel'stv i knigotorgovykh organizatsii', *Kniga*, 31 (1975), 54.

21 *Pechat' SSSR v 1971 godu*, pp. 34, 83–4; *Pechat' SSSR v 1975 godu*, p. 40.

22 *Pechat' SSSR v 1975 godu*, p. 41.

23 Zh. K. Zhandosov & N. N. Grekhovodov, 'Voprosy organizatsii zakazooborota v knizhnoi torgovle', *Izd. delo. Knigovedenie. Ref. inf.*, 1971(8), 58.

24 R. N. Khakimov, 'Ob ustranenii nedostatkov v sisteme knigoizdaniya i knigorasprostraneniya Uzbekistana', *Izd. delo. Knigovedenie. Ref. inf.*, 1972(6), 35.

25 Interview with director of Prosveshchenie, 17 March 1975.

26 'V Goskomizdate SSSR i Ministerstve vysshego i srednego spetsial'nogo obrazovaniya SSSR', *V mire knig*, 1974(11), 25. Not all of these orders would be for textbooks, but the context makes it clear that textbook supply was the chief cause of concern.

27 *Byulleten' Ministerstva vysshego i srednego spetsial'nogo obrazovaniya SSSR*, 1976(9), 32–8.

28 *Spravochnik . . .* (note 4), pp. 42, 46–7.

29 E. Lavrenko & A. Knorre, 'Chemu nauchit takoe uchebnoe posobie?', *Kommunist*, 1975(10), 126–8; and note in *Kommunist*, 1975(13), 128.

30 'Zavtrashnie knigi i nyneshnie zaboty', *V mire knig*, 1973(10), 24–5.

31 N. Velikanova, 'Iz chego skladyvaetsya tsena knigi', *Kn. torgovlya*, 1972(10), 9.

32 V. A. Borisenko, 'Effekt vzaimodeistviya', *V mire knig*, 1975(3), 7.

33 Interview with director of Prosveshchenie, 17 March 1975.

34 D. Zuev, 'Vypusk uchebnikov – na uroven' sovremennykh trebovanii', *Poligrafiya*, 1977(2), 1–2.

35 'V Goskomizdate SSSR', *V mire knig*, 1973(12), 9.

36 *Pechat' SSSR v 1975 godu*, pp. 56–9.

37 L. S. Kharlampiev & N. K. Medvedeva, 'Razrabotka prognoza razvitya knizhnoi produktsii SSSR na osnove dannykh demografii', in *Voprosy ekonomiki i organizatsii truda v poligrafii* (M., 1971), pp. 7–8; and *Pechat' SSSR v 1975 godu*, pp. 56–9.

38 'Opyt knigoizdaniya . . .' (note 7), p. 48.

39 Dinershtein et al. (note 10), p. 19.

40 V. Ezhkov, G. Martirosyan & M. Chetyrkin, 'Vazhnoe zveno propagandy nauchno-tekhnicheskikh dostizhenii', *Kommunist*, 1974(15), 118–19.

41 V. Ezhkov, 'Tekhnicheskaya kniga: spros i propaganda', *V mire knig*, 1974(4), 37, and *Pechat' SSSR v 1971 godu*, pp. 18–23. The percentage of copies reaching the book trade is derived from figures given here for Group 'A' of Soviet book production, defined (ibid., p. iii) as excluding publications for official and internal use. Figures for 1971 are used because books published later would probably not have been classified as 'unsaleable' by 1973.

42 G. Safronov, 'Tirazh opredelit chitatel'', *Kn. obozrenie*, 1977(3), 14–15.

43 B. S. Gorbachevskii, 'Razvitie sredstv nauchnoi i tekhnicheskoi informatsii i knigoizdatel'skoe delo', *Kniga*, 21 (1970), 50.

44 E. S. Likhtenshtein, 'Nauchnoe knigoizdatel'stvo i nauchno-tekhnicheskii progress', in *Materialy pervoi Vsesoyuznoi nauchnoi konferentsii po problemam knigovedeniya* (M., 1971), p. 64.

45 *Pechat' SSSR v 1975 godu*, pp. 43, 94.

46 'Opyt knigoizdaniya . . .' (note 7), p. 48.

47 'Pechatnyi tsekh Rossii', *Kn. obozrenie*, 1974(10), 2.

48 D. Ivanov, 'Nedetskie problemy detskikh knig', *V mire knig*, 1976(3), 10.

49 *Book publishing in the USSR* (Harvard/Oxford, 1972), p. 24.

50 A. N. Kostakov, 'Knizhnaya torgovlya – vazhnyi uchastok ideologicheskoi raboty', *Kn. torgovlya. Issled. i mat.*, vol. 1 (M., 1974), p. 11.

51 *Kniga i chtenie v zhizni nebol'shikh gorodov* (M., 1973), p. 58.

52 Makhov (note 1), p. 22.

53 Ya. I. Arest & V. A. Dobrushin, *Bibliotechnye kollektory* (M., 1973), p. 16, state that the supply agencies' turnover was nearly 63 million roubles in 1970, and that libraries bought books to nearly the same value from bookshops. Book sales in 1970 were 610.5 million roubles (*Kn. torgovlya. Issled. i mat.*, vol. 2 (M., 1975), p. 217), of which 126 million roubles of library purchases would represent 20.6 per cent.

54 B. I. Stukalin, 'Sostoyanie i perspektivy vypuska literatury izdatel'stvami SSSR', *Izd. delo. Ref. inf.*, 1975(6), 11.

55 K. I. Kochin, 'Komplektovanie fondov bibliotek v Rossiiskoi Federatsii', *Kn. torgovlya. Ref. inf.*, 1976(1), 5. The unit of measurement is not stated.

56 I. Fonyakov, 'Dyuma-otets i vnuki Yuriya Petrovicha', *Literaturnaya gazeta*, 2 July 1975, 13.

57 *Voprosy ideologicheskoi raboty KPSS* (M., 1972), pp. 554–9.

58 *Normativnye materialy po izdatel'skomu delu dlya organizatsii ministerstv i vedomstv* (M., 1973), pp. 6–12.

59 V. G. Mochalov, 'Ob uporyadochenii izdaniya vedomstvennoi literatury', *Izd. delo. Knigovedenie. Ref. inf.*, 1972(7), 2.

60 Ibid., pp. 3–4.

61 *Byulleten' Ministerstva vysshego i srednego spetsial'nogo obrazovaniya SSSR*, 1971(5), 14.

62 Ibid., 1975(12), 30–3.

63 *Pechat' SSSR v 1971 godu*, p. 6; ... *v 1974 godu*, pp. 10–11; ... *v 1975 godu*, pp. 10–11.

64 'V Goskomizdate SSSR', *V mire knig*, 1975(9), 5.

65 *Spravochnik normativnykh materialov dlya izdatel'skikh rabotnikov*, 2nd ed. (M., 1977), pp. 85–91.

66 N. Kuznetsova, 'Lipetsskii prezent', *Sovetskaya kul'tura*, 17 June 1975, 3.

67 *Pechat' SSSR v 1971 godu*, p. 13; ... *v 1975 godu*, p. 23.

68 A. H. Brown, 'Moscow – absent friends and unexpected visitors', *Times lit. suppl.*, 11 June 1976, 704.

69 D. M. Sutulov, *Avtorskoe pravo*, 3rd ed. (M., 1974), pp. 146–7.

70 *Sbornik normativnykh materialov po roznichnym tsenam na izdatel'skuyu produktsiyu* (M., 1974), pp. 56–7.

71 Ezhkov et al. (note 40), pp. 116–17.

72 L. S. Kharlampiev, 'Budushchee knigi i knizhnogo dela', in *Vtoraya Vsesoyuznaya nauchnaya konferentsiya po problemam knigovedeniya*, 11 vols. (M., 1974), vol. 6, pp. 3–6; and interview with Director of All-Union Research Institute for Complex Polygraphic Problems, 12 March 1975.

73 Preliminary results are reported in 'O tendentsiyakh vypuska osnovnykh vidov knizhnoi produktsii do 1990g.', *Izd. delo. Ref. inf.*, 1973(5), 8–11.

74 Kharlampiev & Medvedeva (note 37), pp. 3–18.

10. CONCLUSIONS

1 Remarked upon by the director of the Lenin Library in N. M. Sikorskii, 'Osnovnye zadachi issledovaniya chteniya na sovremennom etape', in *Problemy sotsiologii i psikhologii chteniya* (M., 1975), pp. 7–8.

Select bibliography

The bibliography is a selective listing of the more important works on the subjects dealt with, whether or not cited in this book. It is arranged in four sections:
  A. Bibliographies and bibliographical surveys
  B. Serials
  C. Official publications
  D. Other works
Articles appearing in the serials listed in section B are not shown separately, nor are those official regulations which are printed in the collections of documents listed in section C.

A. BIBLIOGRAPHIES AND BIBLIOGRAPHICAL SURVEYS

Dewhirst, M. 'A selective bibliography of works on censorship'. In Dewhirst, M. & Farrell, R. *The Soviet censorship.* Metuchen, 1973, pp. 153–65.

Dinershtein, E. A. *Razvitie izdatel'skogo dela v soyuznykh i avtonomnykh respublikakh. Obzor literatury 1967–1972gg.* M., 1973.

Istrina, M. V. & Smirnova, V. P. *Izdanie massovo-politicheskoi literatury. Obzor literatury (1968–1974).* M., 1976.

Izdatel'skoe delo. Bibliograficheskaya informatsiya. M., 1969– . Monthly. Title varied 1969–72.

Izdatel'skoe delo i problemy knigovedeniya. Ukazatel' otechestvennoi literatury 1970–1974. M., 1975.

'Knigovedenie. Ukazatel' literatury, vypushchennoi v . . . g.' Published in *Kniga* (see section B), covering the following years in the issues stated:
1961–64 in issue 11, 295–334	1970 in issue 25, 196–219
1965–66 in issue 16, 240–70	1971 in issue 28, 199–233
1967 in issue 19, 226–44	1972 (pt 1) in issue 29, 226–57
1968 in issue 21, 248–69	1972 (pt 2) in issue 30, 235–48
1969 in issue 24, 235–55	1973 in issue 31, 195–215

Continuation of 'Sovetskaya literatura . . .', below.

Knizhnaya torgovlya. Bibliograficheskaya informatsiya. M., 1973– . Six issues in 1973 and 1974. Monthly from 1975.

Poligraficheskaya promyshlennost'. Bibliograficheskaya informatsiya. M., 1969– . Monthly.

'Sovetskaya literatura po voprosam knigoizdatel'skogo dela (1945–1960)'. *Kniga,* issue 5, 383–420; issue 6, 372–400; issue 7, 374–416. Continued by 'Knigovedenie . . .', above.

Tyapkin, B. G. *Voprosy tipologii v sovremennom knigovedenii. Obzor literatury 1962–1972.* M., 1974.

155

B. SERIALS

Izdatel'skoe delo. Referativnaya informatsiya. M., 1968– . Monthly. Title varied 1968–72.
Kniga. Issledovaniya i materialy. M., 1959– . Irregular series.
Knizhnaya torgovlya. M., 1963–72. In 1973 amalgamated with *V mire knig.*
Knizhnaya torgovlya. Issledovaniya i materialy. M., 1973– . Irregular series.
Knizhnaya torgovlya. Referativnaya informatsiya. M., 1973– . Six issues in 1973 and 1974. Monthly since 1975.
Knizhnoe obozrenie. M., 1966– . Weekly.
Pechat' SSSR v . . . godu. M., 1954– . Annual.
Poligraficheskaya promyshlennost'. Referativnaya informatsiya. M., 1968– . Monthly.
Poligrafiya. M., 1963– . Monthly. Formerly *Poligraficheskoe proizvodstvo.*
Polihrafiya i vydavnycha sprava. L'viv, 1964– . Irregular series.
Redaktor i kniga. M., 1958– . Irregular series.
V mire knig. M., 1961– . Monthly. Absorbed *Knizhnaya torgovlya* in 1973.

C. OFFICIAL PUBLICATIONS

Normativnye materialy po izdatel'skomu delu dlya organizatsii ministerstv i vedomstv. M., 1973.
O partiinoi i sovetskoi pechati, radioveshchanii i televidenii. M., 1972.
'O stavkakh avtorskogo voznagrazhdeniya za izdanie proizvedenii nauki, literatury i iskusstva'. *Sobranie postanovlenii pravitel'stva RSFSR,* 1975 (9), 148–76.
'Polozhenie o Gosudarstvennom komitete Soveta Ministrov SSSR po delam izdatel'stv, poligrafii i knizhnoi torgovli'. *Sobranie postanovlenii pravitel'stva SSSR,* 1973(23), 547–58.
Sbornik normativnykh materialov po roznichnym tsenam na izdatel'skuyu produktsiyu. M., 1974.
Sovetskaya pechat' v dokumentakh. M., 1961.
Spravochnaya kniga korrektora i redaktora. M., 1974.
Spravochnik normativnykh materialov dlya izdatel'skikh rabotnikov. M., 1969. 2nd ed. M., 1977.
Spravochnik normativnykh materialov dlya rabotnikov knizhnoi torgovli. M., 1970.
'Tipovoi izdatel'skii dogovor na literaturnye proizvedeniya'. *Byulleten' normativnykh aktov ministerstv i vedomstv SSSR,* 1975(7), 34–7.
Trud i zarabotnaya plata rabotnikov izdatel'stv i redaktsii zhurnalov. M., 1973.
Voprosy ideologicheskoi raboty KPSS. Sbornik vazhneishikh reshenii KPSS (1965–1972gg.). M., 1972.
Voprosy ideologicheskoi raboty KPSS. Sbornik dokumentov 1965–1973gg. 2nd ed. M., 1973.

D. OTHER WORKS

Andrianova, N. G. *Analiz khozyaistvennoi deyatel'nosti izdatel'stva.* M., 1971.
Arest, Ya. I. & Dobrushin, V. A. *Bibliotechnye kollektory.* M., 1973.
Barenbaum, I. E. & Davydova, T. E. *Istoriya knigi.* M., 1971.

Bogdanov, N. G. & Vyazemskii, B. A. *Spravochnik zhurnalista.* 3rd ed. Leningrad, 1971.

Book publishing in the USSR. 2nd ed. Harvard/Oxford, 1972.

Bukhgalterskii uchet i kontrol' v knizhnoi torgovle. M., 1974.

Chernyak, A. Ya. *Istoriya tekhnicheskoi knigi. Chast' II. Sovetskii period.* M., 1973.

Chernyi, D. A. *Analiz khozyaistvennoi deyatel'nosti knizhnogo magazina.* M., 1966.

Chertkov, V. L. *Sudebnaya zashchita prav i interesov avtorov.* M., 1971.

Dewhirst, M. & Farrell, R., eds. *The Soviet censorship.* Metuchen, 1973.

Dinershtein, E. A., Belaya, L. A. & Sonkina, F. S. *Sovremennaya praktika pereizdaniya literatury v SSSR.* M., 1972.

Dobkin, S. F., *Osnovy izdatel'skogo dela i knigopechataniya.* 2nd ed. M., 1972.

Ekonomika poligraficheskoi promyshlennosti. M., 1972.

Ezhkov, V., Martirosyan, G. & Chetyrkin, M. 'Vazhnoe zveno propagandy nauchno-tekhnicheskikh dostizhenii'. *Kommunist,* 1974(15), 115–22.

Garibyan, A. M. *Avtorskoe pravo na proizvedeniya nauki.* Erevan, 1975.

Glyazer, L. S. 'Ekonomiko-matematicheskaya model' izdatel'skoi deyatel'nosti'. In *Optimal'noe planirovanie i sovershenstvovanie upravleniya narodnym khozyaistvom.* M., 1969, pp. 423–6.

Gorokhoff, B. I. *Publishing in the USSR.* Bloomington, 1959.

Govorov, A. A. *Istoriya knizhnoi torgovli v SSSR.* M., 1976.

Gunich, T. S. *Ekonomicheskoe stimulirovanie v knizhnoi torgovle.* M., 1974.

Kamyshev, V. G. *Prava avtorov literaturnykh proizvedenii.* M., 1972.

Kharlampiev, L. S. & Medvedeva, N. K. 'Razrabotka prognoza razvitiya knizhnoi produktsii SSSR na osnove dannykh demografii'. In *Voprosy ekonomiki i organizatsii truda v poligrafii.* M., 1971, pp. 3–18.

Kniga i chtenie v zhizni nebol'shikh gorodov. M., 1973.

Kniga i chtenie v zhizni sovetskogo sela. Issue 1– . M., 1972– .

Knyha. Redaktor. Informatsiya. Materialy naukovoi konferentsii. Kyiv, 1973.

Korchagin, B. A. *Material'no-tekhnicheskoe snabzhenie v poligrafii, izdatel'skom dele, knizhnoi torgovle.* M., 1972.

Maio-Znak, E. O. 'Evolyutsiya statistiki pechati v SSSR'. *Sovetskaya bibliografiya,* 1975(3), 3–23.

Malykhin, N. G. *Ocherki po istorii knigoizdatel'skogo dela v SSSR.* M., 1965.

Markus, V. A. *Organizatsiya i ekonomika izdatel'skogo dela.* 3rd ed. M., 1976.

Materialy pervoi Vsesoyuznoi nauchnoi konferentsii po problemam knigovedeniya. M., 1971.

Mil'chin, A. E. *Metodika i tekhnika redaktirovaniya teksta.* M., 1972.

Murray, J. 'The Union of Soviet Writers: its organization and leading personnel 1954–1967'. Unpublished PhD thesis, University of Birmingham, 1973.

Nikitina, M. I. *Avtorskoe pravo na proizvedeniya nauki, literatury i iskusstva,* Kazan', 1972.

Presa Ukrains'koi RSR 1918–1973. Naukovo-statystychnyi dovidnyk. Kharkiv, 1974.

Problemy sotsiologii i psikhologii chteniya. M., 1975.

Rabin, L. Ya. & Lyubimov, A. N. *Ekonomika i planirovanie torgovli knigami.* M., 1968.

Redaktirovanie otdel'nykh vidov literatury. M., 1973.

Roudakov, N. S. & Gringolts, I. A. 'L'agence de l'URSS pour les droits d'auteur (VAAP)'. *Revue internationale du droit d'auteur,* 81 (July 1974), 2–33.

Sidel'nikova, L. B. & Gunich, T. S. *Ekonomika knizhnoi torgovli.* M., 1972.

Sikorskii, N. M. *Teoriya i praktika redaktirovaniya.* M., 1971.

Sostoyanie i perspektivy izucheniya sprosa na knizhnuyu produktsiyu. M., 1974.

Sovetskii chitatel'. Opyt konkretno-sotsiologicheskogo issledovaniya. M., 1968.

Sutulov, D. M. *Avtorskoe pravo. Izdatel'skie dogovory. Avtorskii gonorar.* 3rd ed. M., 1974.

Vtoraya Vsesoyuznaya nauchnaya konferentsiya po problemam knigovedeniya. 11 vols. M., 1974.

Index

Academy of Sciences of the USSR, 58, 92, 113
Academy of Social Sciences, 22, 52
Adamson, Joy, *Pippa's challenge*, 97
advances on fees, 72, 74
All-Union Agency for Authors' Rights, *see* VAAP
All-Union Book Chamber, 17, 45, 47, 121
All-Union Research Institute for Complex Polygraphic Problems, 120
All-Union Theatre Society, 92
All-Union Voluntary Association of Book Lovers, 22
APN, publisher, 59
Artistic Fund, 80
Artists' Union, 49, 76
Association of State Publishing-Houses, 30
associations of printers and publishers, 82–3
ASU–PECHAT', 40, 45–7
atheism, publications on, 106
Atomizdat, publisher, 59
authors, 68–80
   criminal prosecution of, 77
   fees, 7, 13–14, 20, 29, 31, 53–4, 57, 70–5, 77, 103, 105, 110, 127–9
   occupational analysis, 78
   proposals to publishers, 40, 46, 56, 63
   and publication abroad, 70, 75–8
   and publishers, 50–2, 55–8, 69–77, 125
   rights, 68–9
   taxation of, 74, 77–8
author's sheet, xi, 72
automated management systems, 44–7
Avrora, publisher, 101

Bartenev, E., *Taina bytiya cheloveka*, 71

Belarus', publisher, 19
Berezka trading organisation, 93
bibliographies, national, 47
Biblioteka mirovoi literatury dlya detei, 114
Bol'shaya sovetskaya entsiklopediya, 21, 94
bonuses, *see* premia
book trade, 91–101
   collection of orders, 25–6, 43–4, 46, 92, 96
   economic position, 93–5
   and edition sizes, 63–5
   exports, 100–1
   incentives in, 93–4
   and Party, 24–5, 96, 99
   planning, 42–4, 46, 91–3
   publicity, 95
   and publishers, 43–4, 91–3, 95–9, 125
   in the republics, 24–5, 99
   second-hand, 100, 111
books, as a commodity, 7–9, 94, 123
   as an economic force, 8–9
bookselling, *see* book trade
Borisov, O. B. & Koloskov, B. T., *Sovetsko-kitaiskie otnosheniya*, 65
Brezhnev, L. I., 21
budget, state, 11–12, 53, 62, 82
Budivel'nik, publisher, 52

campaigns, publishing for, 23, 26, 105–6
capital investment, 11, 82
censorship, 1, 21, 39, 58, 65–7, 125
Central Committee, *see* Party, Central Committee
Central Wholesale Book Warehouse, 92–4
Chief Administration for Material-Technical Supply, *see* Glavsnabsbyt
Chief Administration for the Book

Trade and Book Propaganda, *see* Glavkniga
children's books, 113–14
  demand for, 9, 100, 114
  output of, 15, 20, 102–3, 113–15, 121, 125
Chukovskaya, Lidiya, 57
collections of articles, *see sborniki*
commissioned publications (*zakaznye izdaniya*), 116–18
Committee for the Press (1965–72), 20, 30, 38, 116
Communist Party, *see* Party
computer-based management systems, 44–7
consumer cooperatives, 24–5, 92, 95, 99–100, 111
contracts, publisher–author, 31, 40, 56–8, 69–72, 76–7
  publisher–book trade, 38, 44, 97–8
  publisher–printer, 44, 83–6
coordination of publications, 35, 37, 39–40, 45–6, 56–7, 105, 118–19
copyright, *see* authors, rights
councils of ministers, 20–1, 28–30, 32, 43, 69, 72
court proceedings, 57, 71, 76–7
criticism, literary and artistic, 20

decision-making, 2–3
demand, 7, 9–11, 15–17, 41–2, 92, 97, 119–21, 124
Department of Propaganda, *see* Party, Department of Propaganda
deposit of report literature, 113, 116
Detskaya entsiklopediya, 99
Detskaya Literatura, publisher, 113, 115
dictionaries, 11, 104
discount, in book trade, 93–5, 98
'domestic' publications, 11, 55, 121
Doyle, Sir A. Conan, *The hound of the Baskervilles*, 90
'drift' (*samotek*), 51, 55
Dumas, A., *The three musketeers*, 100

edition sizes (*tirazhi*), amendments to, 14, 40, 43
  definition, xi
  determination of, 44, 54, 63–5, 112–13, 117
  fees according to, 70, 73
editor, definition, xi

editorial office, definition, xi
editorial preparation plans, 39–40, 62–3, 96, 119
editorial work, 25–6, 50–2, 56–9, 71–2, 104
education, ministries of, 39, 109–10
effectiveness in publishing, 13–15
Ekonomika, publisher, 20, 44, 51, 55, 59, 61
encyclopedias, 11, 72, 104
Engels, F., 6, 66, 94
export of books, 60, 82, 100–1

fees, authors', *see* authors, fees
fiction, demand for, 9, 100, 104–5
  fees for, 72–5
  in libraries, 115
  output of, 15, 103–5, 108, 115, 121, 124–5
  prices for, 11
  translations of, 66, 118
  and Writers' Union, 78–80
five-year plans, 41–2, 88, 102–3
forecasting of demand and output, 17, 41, 46, 119–21
Furman, A. E., *Dialekticheskaya kontseptsiya razvitiya sovremennoi biologii*, 110

Glavkniga, 92–5, 97, 115
Glavlit, 19, 21–2, 39, 65–7, 125
Glavpoligrafizdat, 30
Glavsnabsbyt, 36, 86–9
Glyazer, L. S., 7, 9
Gorokhoff, B. I., 2
Goskomizdat, *see* State Committee for Publishing
Gosplan, *see* State Planning Committee
Gossnab, *see* State Committee for Material–Technical Supply
Great Patriotic War, 106
grif, 110

Higher Party School, 22

Ideological Commission, 20
illustrated works, 10, 104
incentive systems, for book exports, 100–1
  in book trade, 93–4
  in publishing, 12, 54–5, 59–62
information services, 31, 39, 113, 116
Institute of Marxism–Leninism, 52

instructional meetings, 20
Iskusstvo, publisher, 66
Istoriya vtoroi mirovoi voiny, 21
Ivanov, I. V., *Jan Werich*, 66

Journalists' Fund, 80
Journalists' Union, 74, 76, 78, 117
journals, *see* periodicals

Kamenyar, publisher, 85
Kazakhstan, publisher, 36
KGB, 34, 65
khozraschet, in book trade, 93–5
    internal, 24, 55, 61
    in publishing, 8, 12–13, 49
    in supply organs, 87
Khudozhestvennaya Literatura,
    publisher, 115
Kniga-pochtoi, 96
Kolos, publisher, 38, 52

Lenin, V. I., 66, 94
Lenkniga, 95
libraries, books for, 100, 106, 114–
    15
    personal, 151n5
    school, 111, 114
library supply agencies, 26, 93, 109,
    115
licensing contract, 77
Liesma, publisher, 55, 79
Litfond, 80, 92
losses, in book trade, 151
    in publishing, 8, 10, 12–13, 20, 29,
    36, 44, 53, 82, 110–12

manuscript, alteration of, 58, 71–2
    refereeing, 23, 37, 52, 56, 58, 107,
    109, 116
    selection, 22, 25–6, 37, 50–1, 55–9,
    63, 66–7, 70–2, 125–6
Marx, K. H., 6, 66, 94
Marxist–Leninist classics, 25–6, 66,
    94, 104, 108
mass publications, 26, 73, 110, 121,
    125
Mayakovskii, V. V., 21
medical literature, 103
Meditsina, publisher, 52, 87
memoirs, 33
Mezhdunarodnaya Kniga, 101
Ministry of Communications, 91
Ministry of Culture, 30, 115
Ministry of Defence, 92
Ministry of Finance, 20, 38, 62

Ministry of Higher and Secondary
    Special Education, 39, 110, 117
minority languages, works in, 7, 11,
    79, 110
Mir, publisher, 59, 97, 101, 119
Molodaya Gvardiya, publisher, 115
Moscow Polygraphic Institute, 17
Musical Fund, 80
Mysl', publisher, 44, 51, 59, 64

na pravakh rukopisi, 146n4
Nauchno-Tekhnicheskaya Kniga,
    association, 83
nauchnye trudy, *see sborniki*
Nauka, publisher, 83, 92
Nebenzya, A. A., 33
'need' for publications, 9, 17, 124
New Economic Policy, 13, 123
newspapers, *see* periodicals

OGIZ, 30
optimality, 14–15

paper, 86–90
    allocation of, 37, 43, 53, 62, 65,
    88–9, 103, 118
    consumption of, 103, 108
    economy in use of, 16, 60, 85, 89–
    90, 104, 125
    for periodicals, 15, 88
    prices, 10–11
    shortage of, 54, 60, 87–8, 97, 112,
    124–5
    supply of, 41–3, 81–2, 105, 121
partiinost', 6, 56–8
Party, 18–27, 124
    authorising publication, 19, 21,
    26, 116
    and authors' fees, 20, 29
    in book trade, 24–5, 96, 99
    and censorship, 21, 66, 125
    Central Committee, 18–22, 27, 32,
    37–8, 49, 57, 66
    criticism of publications, 105–6,
    110
    Department of Propaganda, 15,
    18–22, 24, 27, 79, 125
    direction of publishing by, 6, 18–
    24, 26–7, 106
    discipline, 24
    educational system, 25, 73
    leaders' statements, 18, 20, 25–6,
    104, 107
    local organisations, 19–20, 22–3,
    27

Party—*cont.*
  and paper supplies, 38
  periodicals, 31
  and personnel selection, 18–19,
    22–4, 26
  in printing industry, 24–5, 81
  as publisher, 25–6
  and publishing-houses, 19, 22–4,
    26–7, 31, 52, 57, 118
  spirit, 6, 56–8
  and Writers' Union, 22, 79
People's Control, 21–2, 49
periodicals, distribution of, 91–2
  foundation of, 19, 113
  priority of, 15, 88, 124–5
  publication in, 70–1
personnel, selection, 18–19, 22–4, 26
  training, 22, 31
Planeta, publisher, 93
planning and incentive system, 11,
  38, 53, 55, 61, 87, 93, 108
planning cycle in publishing, 41–4
planning indicators, 13–14, 53–5, 82,
  86, 93
Politburo, 18
policy, 2–5, 16
political literature, 105–8
  demand for, 107
  editorial work on, 104, 107
  fees for, 73, 105
  limitation on length, 90
  output of, 107–8, 121, 125
  and the Party, 23–5, 105, 107
  see also socio-political literature
Politizdat, publisher, 25, 41, 49, 51–
  2, 59, 83, 107
popular scientific literature, 73, 90,
  121
portfolios, 63
Pravda, newspaper, 64
  publisher, 25–6
premia, 12, 60–2
prices, for books, 8–11, 13, 20, 29,
  31, 38, 62, 94, 98, 103, 112, 119,
  123, 130–6
  for paper, 10–11
  policy, 9–11, 123–4
  for printing work, 10–11, 82
printed sheet, definition, xii
printing, capacity allocation, 43–4,
  53, 62, 82, 84–6, 124
  economics, 21–2, 81–3, 86
  industry, 8, 22, 81–6
  and the Party, 24–5, 81
  planning, 42–4, 46, 81–90

prices, 10–11, 82
production relations, 6–9
profits, in book trade, 93–5
  in printing, 82
  in publishing, 7, 10–13, 25, 36,
    54–5, 60–4, 72, 105, 111–12, 118,
    123
Profizdat, publisher, 24
Progress, publisher, 51, 59, 101, 119
proofreading, 25, 72, 104
Prosveshchenie, publisher, 52, 85,
  89, 108, 111
publication plans, 14–15, 33, 35, 50–
  5, 62–3
  as basis of planning work, 42–4,
    53–5, 82, 84
  and book trade, 96–8
  and incentives, 12, 60
  and printers, 82, 84
  scanning by higher authority, 20,
    31, 33, 35, 40
publicity, in book trade, 95
  by publishers, 64–5
publishers, *see* publishing-houses
publisher's sheet, definition, xii
publishing, capitalist, 7
  as cultural activity, 6, 122
  economics of, 6–15, 35, 82, 123–4
  as ideological activity, 6–9, 20–1,
    123
  as an industry, 6–9, 122–3
  by organisations not publishing-
    houses, 19–21, 38, 66, 109, 113,
    115–18
  policy approach, 2–4, 122
  politics of, 6–17, 122–3
  as production, 6–9
  proportions of literature in, 9–11,
    14–17, 102–3
  in the republics, 12, 36–7, 44, 61,
    63, 75, 83, 108, 114
  role of, 1, 6–17, 120, 122–3
  statistics, 5
  study of, 1–2, 4–5, 122
Publishing-House for Foreign
  Literature, 23
publishing-houses, 48–67, 125–6
  and authors' fees, 73–4, 103
  and book prices, 62, 103
  and book trade, 43–4, 92–3, 95–9,
    125
  and central administration, 48–9,
    53, 102–3
  directors of, 49–51, 57–9, 61–2, 64,
    71

economic position, 10–13, 53–5, 63–4, 75
and edition sizes, 63–5
editorial councils, 50–2, 58, 71
editorial staff, 50–1, 55–9, 61, 66–7, 71–2, 89–90, 104, 119, 125–6
and exports, 100–1
financial plans, 38, 42, 62–3
foundation of, 19, 31, 37
incentive systems, 12, 29, 38, 54–5, 59–62
and paper supplies, 62, 87–9
and the Party, 19, 22–4, 26–7, 31, 52, 57, 118
personnel, 22, 26, 50, 54, 62
planning in, 14, 39, 42–4, 53–5, 62–3, 125
and printers, 82–6
profits, 53–5, 60–4, 72, 105, 111–12, 118
publicity, 64–5
salaries in, 59–62
sales, 53–4, 60–1
superior organs, 14, 48–9, 51, 54–5, 61–3, 84, 98, 126
and Writers' Union, 78–9

quality in publishing, 12–13, 75, 126

Radyans'kii Pis'mennik, publisher, 48
readers, power of, 16–17, 124
reading, 16–17, 114, 123
referees, xii, 23, 52, 56, 58, 107, 109
reference works, 15, 104, 121
reissues, xii, 63, 79
    contracts for, 70, 73
    paper for, 87
    proposals for, 92
    of textbooks, 111
report literature, 113, 116
reviewer, xii
right to publish, 19, 39, 69, 116–17, 124
Romanov, P. K., 22
Russkii Yazyk, publisher, 101

salaries, in publishing-houses, 59–62
sale-or-return transactions, 98
sales, in book trade, 46, 93–5, 97–8, 107
    export, 60, 101
    of printed matter, 15
    by publishers, 53–4, 60–1
samizdat, 1

Sartakov, S. V., 79
sborniki, 90, 113, 116–17
scientific and technical literature, 102–4, 108, 112–13, 119
scientific communism, books on, 106–7
second-hand book trade, 100, 111
secrets, state, 56, 58, 65–6
series, 33, 113
sheet, definition, xii
sheet-copy, xii, 13
socialist competition, 55, 62
socio-political literature, 105–8
    Central Committee decree on, 20, 105
    demand for, 96, 107
    editorial work on, 25–6
    output of, 103, 107–8
    see also political literature
Sovetskaya Entsiklopediya, publisher, 59, 106–7
Sovetskaya Rossiya, publisher, 63
Sovetskii Khudozhnik, publisher, 19, 49
Sovetskii Pisatel', publisher, 57, 78, 115
Sovremennik, publisher, 78
Soyuzkniga, 92–4, 97–8, 100–1
Soyuzpechat', 91–2
speculation, 100
Spros i predlozhenie, 93
staff, *see* personnel
State Arbitration, 38
State Bank, 59
State Committee for Labour and Wages, 30–1, 38, 61
State Committee for Material–Technical Supply, 38, 86
State Committee for Prices, 20, 31, 38
State Committee for Publishing, 6, 29–36, 125–6
    authorising publications, 33, 40, 125
    and authors' fees, 29, 31
    board (*kollegiya*), 29, 32–3, 43, 79
    and book trade, 91–3, 98
    chairman, 28, 32, 76
    chief editorial offices, 33–5, 40, 43
    consultative organs, 19, 31–2
    coordination work, 35, 37, 39, 45–6, 56–7, 105, 118–19
    in demand studies, 17, 41
    departmental structure, 33–6
    and edition sizes, 40, 65
    and incentives, 60–2

State Com. for Pub.—*cont.*
  limits length of books, 90, 110, 117
  local organisation, 14, 30–1, 36–7, 44, 78
  and the Party, 18–19, 26
  planning work, 14–15, 31, 33, 35, 39–47, 102–3, 106
  powers, 28, 30–1
  and printing industry, 24, 32, 81–6
  and publishers, 26, 30–1, 48–9, 53, 102–3
  status, 30
  and supplies, 36, 38, 86–9
  and translations, 119
  and the Writers' Union, 79, 106
State Committee for Publishing, Printing and the Book Trade, *see* State Committee for Publishing
State Committee for Science and Technology, 30, 39, 81, 116
State Committee for the Press (1963–5), 30
State Inspectorate for the Quality of Publications, 82
State Planning Committee, 8, 30, 35–8, 41–3, 60, 62, 81, 86
State Scientific and Technical Library, 119
Statistika, publisher, 59
'Statute on the socialist state publishing-house', 49
Stukalin, B. I., 32
subsidies, 10–13, 20, 35–6, 124
supplies, 36, 38, 86–9, 124
  see also paper
Supreme Court of the USSR, 57, 77
Supreme Soviet, 28

TASS, 68
tastes, formation of, 9, 124
taxation, of authors, 74, 77–8
  of publishers, 12
technical literature, *see* scientific and technical literature
textbooks, 108–12
  demand for, 100, 108–9
  economics of issuing, 12, 110–11
  editorial work on, 104, 109–10
  fees for, 73–4, 109–11
  for higher and special education, 25, 109–11, 116–17
  output of, 15, 38, 102–3, 108
  planning of, 39, 108–9
  prices of, 10–11, 110–11
  revision of, 20–1

  for schools, 10, 108–12
  selection of, 57, 109–10
  stable, 111–12
  thematic plan, definition, xiii
  see also publication plans
tirazh, see edition size
tirazhnye komissii, 65, 96, 109
title, definition, xiii
trade, *see* book trade
trade unions, 38–9, 50, 59, 61
translation, fees for, 71, 75–7, 118, 129
  freedom of, 75–6
  of non-Soviet works, 10, 66, 79, 118–19
  of Soviet works, 75–9, 104
Transport, publisher, 92
Tsentral'no-Chernozemnoe, publisher, 23, 118
Tsentrokoopkniga, 99
Tsentrosoyuz, 99
turnover tax, 12

Udmurtiya, publisher, 79
Ukituvchi, publisher, 108
Ukrainian Soviet Encyclopedia, 59
Union of Journalists, *see* Journalists' Union
Universal Copyright Convention, 2, 23, 70, 76, 118–19
unpriced publications, 17
unsold stock, 17, 98–9, 107, 113

VAAP, 76–7
Vneshtorgizdat, publisher, 59, 101
Voenizdat, publisher, 63
volume, definition, xiii
VUOAP, 76

waste paper, exchange for books, 90, 104
writers, *see* authors
Writers' Union, 78–80, 125
  and authors, 55, 74, 76, 78–80
  and the Party, 22, 79
  and publication plans, 79, 105, 119
  and publishers, 78–9
  and State Committee for Publishing, 79, 106

Yuridicheskaya Literatura, publisher, 56

Zemlya nasha lipetsskaya, 118
Znanie, publisher, 107
Znanie-sila, 21